"10 Steps to Being a Loving Christian Husband and Father"

by

Lee Bayless

Copyright, Lee Bayless

© 2018 by Lee Bayless.

Cover Design:

To contact the author, write to 10 Steps, P.O. Box 797, Choctaw, Oklahoma, 73020 or e-mail lee@10steps.life.

Dedication

This book is dedicated to my loving wife Barbara and my wonderful children Tyler and Madison. They have all blessed my life in so many tremendous ways and their undying support has helped me to succeed as a loving Christian husband and a loving Christian father. I wish every man could be as fortunate to have a strong Christian family surround them.

Acknowledgement

A special thanks to Rev. Ray Sikes, former Senior Pastor at First Baptist Church of Choctaw, OK, for his insight and scripture references that are included in this book. His guidance is greatly appreciated. His friendship is greatly valued.

About the Author

Lee Bayless is one of America's favorite entertainers specializing in clean, family-friendly comedy with a performing career stretching over forty-five years in showrooms, theaters, and cruise ships around the world.

As a writer, Lee won the top award at the International Family Film Festival with his original screenplay TEENAGE ASTRONAUT.

Lee lives in Oklahoma with his wife and their three Golden Retrievers-- Maggie, Scooter, and Bear.

Table of Contents

Introduction To Being A Loving Christian Husband

Introduction To Being A Loving Christian Father

"10 Steps to Being a Loving Christian Husband"

INTRODUCTION
To Being a Loving Christian Husband

This book was written with the assumption that you are a Christian man looking for ways to improve your relationship with your wife and children.

However, that doesn't mean that you must be a Christian to understand the steps contained in this book and in fact, if you are not a Christian, reading this book may help open your heart to accept Jesus Christ as your Lord and Savior.

When God sent His only begotten son to this world, He wanted mankind to have a way to have their sins forgiven and to find the pathway to everlasting life in heaven. That pathway is through being reborn in Jesus Christ and to be baptized in His holy name.

Since the beginning of time, every human being has sin in their heart and God wanted to save mankind from a life of eternity in Hell, so He sent Jesus Christ to die on a cross to take away all of your sins and to wash them from your soul. No matter what sins you may have done, God has given you the ability to repent for your sins and ask forgiveness so that you can start a new life with Jesus Christ and the Holy Spirit living inside of your heart.

"For God loved the world in this way: He gave his one and only Son, so that everyone who believes in him will not perish but have eternal life" (John 3:16 CSB).

Becoming a Christian starts with you professing your belief that Jesus Christ is the Son of God and that you accept him into your heart as your Lord and Savior.

You can do this with a simple prayer like this: "Dear God, I know I have sinned and ask you for your forgiveness. I know you sent your Son Jesus Christ to sacrifice his life to pay for my sins and I gladly accept him as my personal Lord and Savior to live in my heart for all eternity. Thank you for your love and thank you for your forgiveness and thank you for letting me be a part of your Christian family. I pray these things in the name of Jesus Christ. Amen."

If you prayed that prayer and believe it in your heart, you have been forgiven from your sins and have an eternal home prepared for you in heaven.

You are now a Christian man, and it is your responsibility to live the rest of your earthly days as a loving Christian Husband and a loving Christian Father.

The United States has the dubious title of "Divorce Capital of the World." There are numerous factors that contribute to the high rate of divorce, such as job stress, alcohol addiction, drug addiction, adultery, boredom, grief, spousal abuse, and more.

But each of these relationship issues has something in common—they are human traits of weakness that should not be present in a happy, loving marriage.

Even if challenges are present, marriage is an ever-changing relationship that should be able to overcome all odds so long as the couple can communicate and work together to solve their problems.

Why do marriages not last as long as they used to? Psychologists and statisticians can formulate some interesting theories, such as too much television, longer working hours, and more stress, but at the end of the day, divorce happens because one or both partners decide life is better without the person they have taken their vows of marriage with.

Some people believe it is often easier to just give up and start all over instead of working through the problems to save their marriage.

If you are lucky enough to find someone you love so much that you marry them, how could you ever allow that love to sputter out to the point that your marriage ends in divorce?

Today's world is a plastic world. People have been taught that if something breaks, you simply throw it away and get another one. Unfortunately, many people view marriage the same way.

A divorce is usually not a fifty-fifty decision between both people. Unfortunately, when one spouse wants out of the marriage for one reason or another, the other spouse is forced to make a difficult decision.

One choice is to accept the situation of an impending divorce and give up. Another choice is to go through counseling and try to save the marriage. But that takes a willing partner, which is a long shot since that partner is the one wanting a divorce in the first place.

Hopefully, keeping focused on being a loving Christian husband will help you maintain and enjoy a healthy marriage, and you will never be faced with a divorce.

I do know this: A marriage just doesn't fall apart overnight and ends up in divorce court the next day. It takes time for a marriage to fall apart. And if you watch your marriage carefully, you can notice the small changes and do something about them before they move past the tipping point and beyond repair.

Say you look at yourself in the mirror and you are happy with your size, shape, and weight. If you take care of yourself, you will remain satisfied with what you see.

But if you don't take care of yourself, you can start to put on extra weight—only a few pounds here and there—and if you continue to ignore the changes in your body, you can soon find yourself with an extra twenty or thirty pounds around your belly.

If you don't address the expanding problem, your weight will balloon to the point that it might seem impossible to reverse, and you'll just accept the unwanted change, figuring that it's too late to do anything about it, and continue to live an unhealthy life. It's much easier to just do nothing at all than try to solve your problem, but hoping the situation will get better is not a realistic solution.

Not only does this affect how you feel about yourself, but it also causes drastic damage to your body.

But let's say you look in the mirror regularly, and as soon as you notice that you're five pounds heavier than normal, you start to get the problem under control. You start to eat healthier, walk more, do some exercises, and before you know it, the weight begins to disappear. Dealing with five pounds is a lot easier than dealing with fifty pounds. If you really want to fix a problem, don't ignore its existence—fix it immediately.

Your relationship with your wife is the same way. If you continually examine your marriage and fix the small problems as they arise, they will never become so large that you can't resolve them, leaving you to live a more peaceful life.

However, if you just ignore the small problems, they can build up and fester until they reach a boiling point that is almost impossible to solve without professional counseling or outside help. Small problems that remain unresolved can easily lead a married couple to seek a divorce.

Divorce is a tragic affair that not only affects husbands and wives but also affects their children and other family members. The emotional fallout from a failed marriage can have devastating ripple effects that extend to many people beyond the couple at the center of the problem.

Children of divorced parents have emotional baggage thrust upon them that can cause severe behavioral problems. In today's world, it's hard enough to be a child anyway, but adding divorce to that equation is a challenge that no child should have to face.

So often, children mistakenly believe they are the ones at fault for their parents' deteriorating marriage. They become pawns in their parents' power struggle and are often forced to choose favorites, causing them extreme (and unnecessary) hardship.

There are two ways to ensure you will never experience the pain and unintended consequences of divorce. The first way is to never get married. There are some people who have no desire to enter a marriage. They say they are happy being single forever, but truth be told, they are missing one of the most joyful experiences in the world by not having a soul mate to share their life with. Also, God intended for us to be married, as He tells us in the Bible:

"This is why a man leaves his father and mother and bonds with his wife, and they become one flesh" (Genesis 2:24 CSB).

The second (and best) strategy that ensures you will never have a divorce is to be a loving Christian husband and marry a woman who feels the same way as you do about the sanctity of marriage.

This means that you will need to have some honest, frank conversations with the woman you would like to marry BEFORE you marry her or have children with her. It might seem a bit embarrassing at first to discuss your feelings about marriage with your chosen woman, but a few moments of initial embarrassment are far less painful and emotional than uncovering "irreconcilable differences" after the fact and resorting to divorce as the ultimate solution.

Unlike our female counterparts, most men don't dream about fairytale weddings and having a great wife and kids. It might cross their minds every now and then, but men don't dream about marriage like women do.

Most of the guys I knew when I was growing up simply met a girl and dated her until the girl started talking about marriage. Then after getting some family pressure from his and her parents alike, they'd finally propose and get married. And it wasn't too long after that when they'd discover that dating a girl and being married to her are two completely different things.

Unfortunately, there's not a lot of practical advice floating around about how to be a good husband or how to maintain an exciting, long-lasting marriage.

Many men simply learn by trial and error how to try and be good husbands as they progress through marriage, but the immense pressure of being a husband, a father, and a provider can make the process neither fun nor fulfilling and overwhelming at times.

This book was written to give men some easy-to-follow steps so that they can learn how to be loving Christian husbands.

The steps in this book will <u>not</u> give you instructions for changing your wife. You don't fall in love and marry someone to change them. Rather, these steps will help you examine your own role as a man and as a husband so that you will have a happy, healthy Christian marriage for the rest of your life.

You cannot change your wife. You should not try to change your wife. That doesn't mean that your wife is incapable of change, but she will only make changes in herself if she wants to, not because you want her to or ask her to.

When she notices the positive changes in you that will come because of you following the steps in this book, your wife will respond accordingly, and her love and respect for you is sure to grow stronger.

Both you and your wife will change naturally as your marriage progresses through the years, but the one thing that should never change is your belief in God. Keep your marriage centered on your faith and you will remain a loving Christian husband throughout your life.

Remember this: the only thing that you can change in your marriage is yourself.

If you try your best to be a great Christian husband, your wife will appreciate your efforts and will learn to reciprocate by being a great wife.

The result will be beneficial to you both as you live a healthy, nurturing, harmonious marriage that will last through all the days of your life.

Step 1
SHARE GOD WITH YOUR WIFE

If you want to honor God's plan for you and your wife, then you need to make sure that the two of you share God with each other since it is by God's grace and special touch that you both exist. Your marriage should involve God in as many ways as possible. You should have a church home together. You should feel free to openly discuss God's impact on you and your wife. You should share prayers together. Read the Bible together. Raise Christian children together.

"Husbands, in the same way, live with your wives with an understanding of their weaker nature yet showing them honor as coheirs of the grace of life, so that your prayers will not be hindered" (1 Peter 3:7 HCSB).

How many times have you channel-surfed through the TV stations and said, "There's just nothing good on any of these channels" Next time that happens, turn the TV off and open your Bible. Don't make any plans, just open your Bible to a random location and begin reading a Scripture. You will be surprised at how the Lord will guide you to a verse that somehow has meaning at that time of your life.

When you select a random Scripture like this, it does a few good things. First, it removes the boredom of mindlessly scanning through TV channels, which are usually full of negative content anyway.

Second, it brings God's Word to the forefront of your marriage and changes your thoughts to positivity.

Third, it causes you to interact personally with your wife and for both of you to share God with each other.

Keep a Bible near your favorite chair. I'm not a betting man, but if I were, I might wager that most people could find their TV remote faster than they could find their Bible. How about you? Do you keep your Bible in a dusty bookcase somewhere but keep the TV remote next to your favorite chair?

Move your Bible closer to your life and read it as often as you can. Make it a regular part of your daily routine to discuss Bible verses with your wife.

As the spiritual leader of your family, it is your responsibility to bring religion into your marriage. Do not wait for your wife or your children to suggest it. This is your job as the man of the house to share God's Word with your wife.

Some people get bashful when faced with talking about God. They don't want to be known as the "religious guy" that's always preaching to everyone. But that's exactly what God wants us to do, to share the word of God with the world.

"No one, after lighting a lamp, covers it with a basket or puts it under a bed, but puts it on a lampstand so that those who come in may see its light" (Luke 8:16 CSB).

That doesn't mean that you have to make every conversation a heavy, religious discussion, but you should feel comfortable talking about the Bible with others. If you don't feel comfortable talking about the Bible, it might be because you aren't that familiar with the Word of God. You should spend some time reading the Bible. It amazes me how some people know so many sports statistics but are at a loss when it comes to talking about the Bible and how it relates to them personally.

Share prayers with your wife. Pick a time of day where you both can share some quiet time with each other. Do not be bashful about praying with your wife. It is okay for you to ask for good things to happen in your marriage. It is okay to ask for God's help. It is important for you to hear your wife's prayers, just as it is important for her to hear yours.

That way, you can both feel closer to each other by sharing your feelings and personal desires.

The closer you can feel to each other through sharing God and prayers, the stronger your marriage and relationship will be. This is the foundational basis for you to establish yourself as a loving Christian husband. This is your duty and yours alone. You must want to be a loving Christian husband and work hard to make it a priority in your life.

Your wife must feel comfortable knowing that you are willing to be the spiritual leader of your relationship. Once she feels that comfort level with you, she will find it easier to fulfill her role as your loving Christian wife.

"Wives, submit to your own husbands as to the Lord, for the husband is the head of the wife as Christ is the head of the church. He is the Savior of the body. Now as the church submits to Christ, so wives are to submit to their husbands in everything. Husbands, love your wives, just as Christ loved the church and gave Himself for her to make her holy, cleansing her with the washing water of the word" (Ephesians 5:22–26 HCSB).

You have been given a mandate by God to ensure that your family follows the truth of the Bible. Have you ever read the Bible from start to finish? If not, you should set a goal and start reading God's Holy Word. In all honesty, it's a long task to read the Bible, but there are several reading plans available online for you to choose from so that you can follow a structured path through the Holy Scriptures. It's not how fast you can read it, it's what you learn with every turn of the page.

Some of the reading plans guide you to completion in ninety days while other plans can take a year or more. There are plans that focus on the Old Testament and others that focus on the New Testament.

No matter how long it takes, you owe it to yourself to read the entire Bible. Your eternal life depends on it.

In the Bible, you will learn the truth, and once you know the truth, it is your responsibility to live the way of the truth. If you have read the truth and then choose not to follow it, you are on a direct path to disobeying God's Word and will be doomed to hell.

As you share God with your wife, you should do all you can to set a righteous course for your wife and family. It is up to you to set the tone so that everyone understands your leadership role.

That means leading prayers at meals, conducting Bible study, and getting you and your family to church on time.

Go to church with your wife at every opportunity and you will begin to share the strength of the Lord in your relationship. Be open about your religious feelings with your wife so that she can get to know you better on a spiritual level. Merely going to church with your wife only scratches the surface of a spiritual relationship with your wife.

Find a Sunday school class that has other couples that are your age and become active participants. Don't sit quietly in the corner and be a passive observer. You'll get out of your class what you put into it, so participate. Answer questions, volunteer to read Scripture, introduce your wife and yourself to others in the class, welcome new visitors, and show an interest in them.

This might take a little getting used to. Some people are shy in this type of setting. Try to be friendly and you will soon discover how many new friends you can meet. The comfort of having the support of an entire Bible class can be a welcome thing, especially during a time of personal need. There will be times to share prayer requests, personal problems, community needs, and all sorts of other requests that can oftentimes be solved more easily in a group setting.

Take advantage of the help that others are willing to offer. This doesn't mean taking unfair advantage of others, but it does mean accepting help when it is offered. People in your church are loving Christians who want to help others in need. You should be the same way and offer to help others every chance you get. How many times have you heard the saying, "It is better to give than receive"? You really begin to understand this when you become a true giver to others. Do something nice for people you don't know, and you will feel the positive change inside your heart knowing you are making the world a better place.

When your wife sees that you are offering to help others, her respect and admiration will grow for you and give her a sense of pride that she is married to a loving Christian husband. She will also follow your lead and (if she's not already) will soon be sharing God with others as you have with her.

"To sum up, each one of you is to love his wife as himself, and the wife is to respect her husband" (Ephesians 5:33 CSB).

Step 2
DEVOTE YOURSELF TO YOUR WIFE

Have you ever watched a poker tournament on TV? Have you ever heard the phrase "I'm all in"?

In poker terms, this means that you are willing to invest everything you have in the strength of your hand. You believe what you have is better than what someone else has and you are willing to risk it all to gain everything in return.

When you are a loving Christian husband, you must be "all in" with your marriage for the rest of your life. You have determined that your wife is the best that there is and that you are willing to bet everything that you have on the strength of your marriage.

When you devote yourself to your wife, you are making a statement with God as your witness that you will honor and protect your wife above all else. The feeling you will get from devoting yourself to this mission will be a tremendous surge of pride. You will reap the rewards of putting your wife on a pedestal of praise so that she feels like the luckiest woman in the world.

"In the same way, husbands are to love their wives as their own bodies. He who loves his wife loves himself. For no one ever hates his own flesh but provides and cares for it, just as Christ does for the church, since we are members of his body" (Ephesians 5:28–30 CSB).

When you can make your wife feel that she is truly the light of your life, then she in turn will open and share with you the feelings of love that burn deep inside her heart. Every woman who dreams of getting married also dreams of finding a perfect Prince Charming to be her knight in shining armor. The next time you look in the mirror, have an honest conversation with yourself to find out how you can adjust your behavior that will help you become a great husband and a hero in your wife's eyes.

If you have been married for a while, you know by now what your wife wants from you. Do you leave your clothes lying all over the bedroom? Do you leave the toilet seat lid up? Do you make the bed? Do you empty the dishwasher or clean the kitchen? You probably know a few little things you do, or don't do, that always irk your wife.

Take a piece of paper and make a list of the things that your wife always has to remind you about. Be honest with yourself and you will no doubt find several things that always cause a little friction in your relationship.

Locating these little flash points makes it a whole lot easier to isolate and eliminate them, freeing you from repeatedly getting upset over the same things time after time.

Examine your list one item at a time and think about why these things are important to your wife and why you've refused or been unmotivated to change. An argument over a friction point only has three real solutions:

She is right. You are wrong.

You are right. She is wrong.

You are both right and neither of you surrenders.

There is a fourth solution, which is to simply ignore the problem and assume that it will sort itself out. But this book is about taking personal responsibility as a Christian husband, and that requires a more proactive resolution.

Notice that in both #1 and #2 above there is an obvious winner and loser. One person conquers the other. Also keep in mind that most people don't like losing (especially to a significant other), so whenever you resort to solutions #1 or #2, there will always be some hurt and wounded feelings on the part of the loser. And if it's not bad enough being the loser, the winner is so glad to have finally won that they may make the loser feel even worse about not winning.

Neither of these solutions are mutually satisfactory since they cause a rift in the relationship that always takes some time to heal. No matter how small the disagreement, any negativity has a definite effect on how well you get along with your wife.

Addressing the flash point directly with your wife and finding a mutually rewarding solution will always be the best for you both. But to address the flash points, you have to identify and address them early on before they become exploding points.

If you are driving your car and you hear a strange grinding noise coming from one of the tires, shouldn't you pull over to assess the problem and try to fix it before it causes an enormous repair bill? You should do the same thing with your marriage. Pay attention to the things that are causing a small amount of friction in your relationship and try to fix them one at a time. Each little problem might not seem important, but if there are several small problems in your relationship, they can all be combined into a larger problem that seems more dramatic than it should be.

Does your wife have a job or watch your children all day? Maybe she is just as tired as you are after a long day and needs your help to do some extra work around the home.

If you come home from work and immediately plop down on the couch to play video games while there are dirty dishes in the sink, she won't think highly of your decision to forego pitching in to help. She'll be upset enough that she won't care that you have had a hard day too and are simply enjoying a little downtime for yourself. She will only see that you have left the hard work for her while you lie around and take it easy.

It's important for you to recognize that most women have different expectations of cleanliness and orderliness than men do. Obviously, there are exceptions to every rule, but usually women want things put in their place and want their home to look orderly at all times. If you know that your wife likes the house to look a certain way and you are not helping out, your wife will feel resentment that you aren't mindful of her preferences. When your wife feels dishonored like this, she will not be in the kind of loving, romantic mood that you might prefer.

What happens is that you feel resentment because your wife is not being who you want her to be for you, while at the same time, she feels resentment because you are not being who she wants you to be for her. This always leads to a mutual standoff, hurt feelings, irritability, and neither one of you feeling good about the other. As a result, you both end up going to bed mildly angry at one another, only to wake up grouchy and start the next day off embroiled in the same conflict.

"Don't let the sun go down on your anger, and don't give the devil an opportunity" (Ephesians 4:26–27 CSB).

Let's change one small detail in the previous story and then replay the scenario. You get home from work, but instead of plopping into your favorite chair, maybe this time you turn on the TV and let it play in the background while you take a few minutes to empty the dishwasher and deal with the dirty dishes in the sink. This shouldn't take too long. I don't mean you have to do it every time you walk in the door, but someone has to deal with the dishes, right?

I know that it's not fun cleaning the kitchen. That's why your wife gets angry when she comes home to a sink full of dirty dishes—because you have inadvertently made the decision that it's her job to clean the kitchen. She will resent you mentally for forcing her to do it. Unfortunately, there's no marriage vow that divides housework into his and her duties. So, devote yourself to making your wife happy by making an effort to clean the kitchen in whatever small ways you can—putting away the dishes, wiping down the counters, making sure the sink is free of dirty dishes, and I promise you she will notice the difference as soon as she walks in the door.

Now, when it's time to turn in for the night, your wife will no longer harbor anger or resentment, and she will be in a more romantic, loving mood. You will rest better and wake up happier and ready to start a new day as a loving Christian husband.

And what did you have to invest? A few minutes of cleaning the kitchen. Wasn't it worth the investment of your time in order to make your household a happier place?

Examine your list of flash point items and try to remedy them one by one. By devoting yourself to your wife, you must try your hardest to make living her life with you a joyful experience. She did not become your wife so that you could have a housekeeper, a cook, a garbage collector, a nanny, and a concubine.

She became your wife because she wanted a loving Christian husband to share her life with, who would do everything he could to make her life enjoyable and meaningful. Do your best to live up to her expectations and give her the man she wants to have in her life.

Devote yourself to your wife by helping with the things she needs to make her happy. You will be rewarded by her devotion to you. Both of you will be happier and enjoy the mutually rewarding relationship that will emerge from your efforts.

Step 3
LOVE YOUR WIFE UNCONDITIONALLY

When you have unconditional love for your wife, you love her no matter what. Period.

She's not perfect. In fact, brace yourself for this news flash: You aren't perfect either. Nobody is perfect. There are countless things that are going to bother you from time to time about your wife, but you have to be able to see past those things and see inside her heart to find the lady that you absolutely love.

If there is something your wife does that is very bothersome to you, of course you can always talk to her about it. But think it through first. Is the thing that's bothering you so important that you want to run the risk of offending your wife? Because no matter how understanding your wife might seem when you talk to her about whatever your concern may be, she will be hurt by your comments, and it will take some time to heal the wounds you will open.

Nobody likes to be told they are doing something wrong. Maybe you don't like the smell of a perfume your wife just bought? Maybe she drinks too much coffee and sometimes has "coffee breath?" Maybe she leaves her makeup on your side of the sink? This list could go on and on. And believe me—she could make a long list of things she doesn't like about you either.

If there is something you want to talk to her about, you might plan to have a solution ready at the same time. Don't just tell your wife, "Wow, that perfume you are wearing sure is strong." You're inviting an argument for no reason because she wouldn't have bought the perfume in the first place if she didn't like it. By vocalizing your disapproval, you have inadvertently told her she doesn't have any taste in perfume. Even if that's not what is communicated, that's what she'll hear. Before you blurt out a critical comment, try approaching it from another angle.

"Be kind to one another, tenderhearted, forgiving one another, as God in Christ forgave you" (Ephesians 4:32 ESV).

If you don't like the perfume she is wearing, buy her a different bottle of perfume that you might prefer and have it ready to give to her. Let her know as politely as you can that her perfume "doesn't match her beauty," but that you found one that might be close. Have your new perfume wrapped nicely as a gift. Be thoughtful in how you approach your wife so that she doesn't get offended or become defensive. When you try to lessen the pain that comes with telling someone they are doing something that bothers you, a little forethought can go a long way to make the situation easier for both of you to handle.

Unconditional love covers all areas. Love your wife for how she acts, how she talks, how she dresses, how she cooks, how she drives, how she raises your kids, and how she makes you feel. The bottom line is that you will have to alter your own feelings to love your wife unconditionally.

By loving your wife unconditionally, you will become her safety zone. Your wife will learn over time that you will be there for her no matter what, and that will give her confidence to be open with you.

When you can have an open dialogue with your wife, nothing can compare. Your wife is the ideal partner in your life to share everything with. God formed the husband/wife relationship to provide a lifelong foundation of earthly support and love that cannot be shaken. As difficult as opening up might seem to be, once you begin to feel comfortable enough to share your innermost thoughts and feelings with your wife, the more you will feel secure in your love for each other.

"Who can find a capable wife? She is far more precious than jewels. The heart of her husband trusts in her, and he will not lack anything good. She rewards him with good, not evil, all the days of her life" (Proverbs 31:10–12 HCSB).

Building that bond is one of the most important things you can accomplish in your marriage. Whether you are a newlywed or have been married for a long time, you should not hesitate to sit down with your wife and profess a desire to have an open dialogue that both of you can depend on for all time. This dialogue should remain confidential between the two of you unless you both agree that certain conversations are okay to share with others, such as an upcoming pregnancy or an illness.

God loves you unconditionally. No matter what you have done in the past, once you ask God for forgiveness, your sins are washed away through the blood of Jesus Christ. If God can love you unconditionally, how hard can it be for you to love your wife the same way? There are going to be difficult times in your marriage, just as there are in all marriages. But the foundation of unconditional love that you build with your wife will allow both of you to forgive one another and move past the difficult times. "Maintain an intense love for each other, since love covers a multitude of sins" (1 Peter 4:8 HCSB).

Marriage should be forever, and you owe it to yourself and to your wife to do all you can to work through all problems that arise in your marriage. Having your marriage based on the love of God will help you build a successful future together so that you will always be able to give her your unconditional love.

Step 4
ALLOW YOUR WIFE TO BE WHO SHE WANTS TO BE

People change. They discover new things. They develop new friendships, new hobbies, new likes and dislikes.

The one thing you can be assured of in your marriage is that both you and your wife will change in many ways. Marriage is a lifelong journey of adapting to changes in yourself and in your wife.

So far in my own marriage, my wife has worked as a travel agent, a sales manager, a cruise ship hostess, a cruise director, a travel agency owner, a director of sales for a cruise line, a school teacher, a private tutor, a full-time mom, and she recently earned her doctorate degree as a reading specialist for children with dyslexia.

In looking at her list of occupations, you might think that she could never hold a job, but she was exceptional at every occupation she ever held. For a variety of reasons, she just felt the need to change her professional direction several times. Sometimes it was to seek a new challenge, other times it was so that she might be able to spend more time at home with our children, but no matter the reason or her direction, I felt it was important for me to support her 100 percent and allow her to be what she wanted to be.

If you are fortunate enough to have a loving relationship with your wife, the last thing you ever want to do is make her feel as if you are controlling her or preventing her from accomplishing her own goals in life. When a person feels confined, they will fight tooth and nail to free themselves. Imagine if you were locked in a small room with no obvious way out. You would start to feel claustrophobic and either fight your way free or stay where you are and turn inward, perhaps even growing emotionally scarred or severely depressed.

Your wife has a brain, a heart, and feelings exactly like you do. In fact, which is part of the reason you fell in love with her in the first place. Men are attracted to women who are exciting to be around. To maintain a wonderful relationship with your wife, you should do all you can to allow her to be excited about who she is and who she wants to be. Don't you want a wife who's as motivated and industrious as the woman described in Proverbs 31?

"First thing in the morning, she dresses for work, rolls up her sleeves, eager to get started. She senses the worth of her work, is in no hurry to call it quits for the day" (Proverbs 31:17–18 MSG).

At the same time, you should be exciting to your wife and excited about who you are and what you want to be. You are never stuck in an endless job unless you choose to remain stuck. Sure, it might be a bit of a hardship to leave a job and retrain yourself for a new profession. But you have to do whatever will make you the happiest. The excitement of taking on a new challenge can also invigorate your personality so that your whole life is recharged.

Learn to accept that your wife is going to have life-changing moments that will require your support. If you choose not to support her or make her feel bad about her desire to make a change in her life, you will do a great disservice to your marriage. Don't be afraid of the change. It might seem as if your wife isn't considering your emotions or your wishes. If you think this, you need to re-examine your personal insecurities because your wife should be able to do whatever she wants to make herself a better person. And so should you.

There are obvious limitations, of course. If your wife wants to start a new business that requires using all your savings and retirement funds, this will obviously jeopardize your family's security and will need to be carefully considered by both of you.

Don't say no immediately if you aren't immediately sold on something your wife wants to pursue. Instead, let her know you understand she wants to make some changes and that while you support her wishes, you want to look at other ways to finance her pursuits without risking your family's security. There are small business loans for females and minorities for which she could apply. There are also numerous government grants and programs for business start-ups by women. Help her move forward. Don't be the one that holds her back, or she will resent you for not being on her side or resent you for being an unsupportive husband. She might not tell you she resents you, but she will internalize her despair that you were not there for her when she needed you. When she is adrift, be a life preserver, not an anchor. Don't make her feel alone.

Sometimes, when a person wants to make a change, they want to move forward quickly without a lot of planning and thought simply because the excitement of doing something new is very alluring. Urge your wife to consult others in the same field, seek job counselors, or use government resources so that she can make the best plans possible that will help ensure her success.

"Without consultation, plans are frustrated, but with many counselors, they succeed" (Proverbs 15:22 NASB).

Whatever you do, be supportive of her wishes and give her the freedom to succeed. By being on her side, you will demonstrate that you are her rock-solid partner. When your wife knows that she has your full support, she will be more confident in her new endeavor, and she will have even more personal drive to succeed because she wants to make you proud of her while she's fulfilling her own self-pride.

If your wife manages to be a success in her new endeavor, you will both reap the rewards of her efforts. If for some reason she falls short of her goals, don't take an "I told you so" attitude. In fact, if you are supporting her the whole time, she will never feel that you were betting against her, and there will be no personal animosity directed at you if she fails.

If, on the other hand, you were hesitant about her new direction and a naysayer all along, and then she does in fact fail, she will resent you for not being on her side. Defeat is a hard pill to swallow, and if your wife faces defeat, who will she have to turn to for solace if you were against her in the first place?

Be the kind of loving Christian husband that is proud and supportive of your wife in all that she does, and she, in turn, will use your love and support to achieve her dreams. The world is hard enough for your wife to battle through without your opposition added to the mix.

Here are some "Dos and Don'ts" for your consideration:

Do develop positive statements of support and use them generously as your wife undertakes her new endeavors.

Do allow her to blossom under your loving support.

Do be involved in her new direction.

Do ask questions and offer suggestions.

Do offer your help and assistance wherever needed.

Don't be negative in words or actions.

Don't dwell on setbacks.

Don't make your wife feel she is doing this alone.

Don't ignore her pleas for help.

Don't try to control her project.

Don't stand in her way.

A loving Christian husband will not only allow his wife to be who she wants to be, but he will also help and assist her any way that he can—physically, mentally, and spiritually.

The bond that is formed through this loving partnership will be a blessing to your wife, and she will understand that you are her biggest fan and supporter.

She will succeed because of you, not in spite of you.

Step 5
KEEP YOUR VOWS SACRED FOREVER

If you make a promise, do you keep it? Do people know you as a man who keeps his word?

"When a man makes a vow to the LORD or takes an oath to obligate himself by a pledge, he must not break his word but must do everything he said" (Numbers 30:2 NIV).

When you look in the mirror, only God and you know the truth about yourself. It's not possible to lie to yourself or to God, so if you are married or planning to be married, you should understand that your wife isn't the only one you are accountable to when it comes to honoring your vows. You're also making a commitment to yourself and to God.

You will be tempted many times in your life to break your sacred vows. The devil delights in tempting you to join his team of sinners. Those temptations are usually triggered and intensified by other negative behaviors, such as drinking or drugs, both of which can cloud your judgment. When you can't think clearly, you're at risk of making decisions that can have an extremely negative effect on you and your wife.

If you break your vows and succumb to adulterous behavior or thoughts, you are not only committing a sin but also betraying the promise you made to yourself, to your wife, and to God. For the few brief moments of physical pleasure that you might get from an illicit relationship, you'll be sacrificing years of love and trust.

Not only does adultery ruin the trust between you and your wife, but you also run the risk of catching sexually transmitted diseases that can cause extreme discomfort, embarrassment, or even kill you. It doesn't matter if you use protection or not. Many STDs can be transmitted through numerous ways. Catching these diseases yourself is traumatic enough, but many unfaithful men have unknowingly infected their wives with the same disease they have.

Sexual relations with a person other than your wife is a sin against God and inevitably leads to severe marital problems. All the time and love you have invested in your marriage can vanish in one illicit instant. You can lose everything you have worked for in the blink of an eye, in one moment of weakness. Your wife, your children, and your self-respect should always be at the forefront of your thoughts. What kind of an example are you setting by your actions?

"You have heard that it was said, Do not commit adultery. But, I tell you, everyone who looks at a woman to lust for her has already committed adultery with her in his heart. If your right eye causes you to sin, gouge it out and throw it away. For it is better that you lose one part of your body than for your whole body to be thrown into hell. And if your right hand causes you to sin, cut it off and throw it away. For it is better that you lose one part of your body than for your whole life to depart into hell!" (Matthew 5:27-30 BSB).

With all the techno-gadgets and personal devices now available in the world, there are more ways than ever for individuals to view nude, lewd, pornographic images. A simple Internet search can yield hundreds or thousands of photos and videos geared toward a specific desire. It's easier than ever to sin with just the simple click of a mouse button.

Sin that's easy to access anonymously doesn't make it any less sinful. Porn addiction exists in the world now more than ever before and likely correlates to the rise of sexual assaults and lack of respect for females.

Since pornography can be concealed within an electronic device, it's easy to think that it's a safe, victimless way to appease personal fantasies. In reality, pornography is a violent, abusive, degrading spectacle that enables perverts to prey on others and allows Satan to control their thoughts and actions.

When the mind and body are consumed with pornographic images, the heart lusts for carnal sin, and according to the Scriptures, this is considered adultery. It's not necessary to have physical interaction with another person to commit adultery—it is as easy as watching someone else and wishing to be with them sexually. If your heart desires illicit relations and you enable those desires by viewing pornography, you are not being faithful to your wife and you are sinning in the eyes of the Lord.

But what if your wife wants to watch pornography with you? Then both of you are not faithful to each other. You need to be able to find excitement with your wife based on your own personal interactions with each other, not by bringing strangers and lewd behavior into your intimate relationship.

The surest way to avoid the temptations of adultery is to remove yourself from situations that enable that type of behavior in the first place. Bars, nightclubs, bachelor parties, weekly poker games, guys' night out—unless you are with a group of other like-minded Christian men, the fact remains that when a group of men get together for a guys' night out, they like to drink, smoke, gamble, and go to clubs—all of which can lead to situations that can be very compromising for a loving Christian husband.

If you are a strong Christian, your non-Christian friends will take delight in sending temptation your way. The devil loves to tempt those who believe. They will do things as a joke, not intending to really tempt you, but if you put yourself in a compromising situation, you can be assured that you will be tempted to participate through peer pressure. If your friend is having a bachelor party at a strip club, no doubt you will be labeled as the "Goody Two-shoes" of the group and an extra effort will be made to send female companionship your way.

In an environment like this, excess alcohol and scantily clad women can be almost too much for anyone to resist. The best thing you can do is to avoid situations like this whenever possible. A good rule of thumb is to ask yourself, *Would I be doing this if my wife were here with me?*

Another strong deterrent is to think about how you would feel if your wife were doing the same thing without your knowledge. Even if you don't physically participate in any of the strip club activities, according to the Bible as previously discussed, the simple act of looking at another woman with lewd thoughts in your mind is the same as adultery.

If you are honest with yourself, how many times have you seen an attractive lady pass by and immediately let that physical attraction consume your thoughts? It's difficult not to.

However, once you are married, you must learn to tame the mental beast inside of you. That doesn't mean that you have to stop admiring beautiful women as they pass by. But it does mean that you should be able to halt your admiration at a certain point before it passes into mental pornography and lewd thoughts. God will always make beautiful ladies, and they will still attract your attention. But if you are married, you need to remain mentally faithful to your wife as much as you remain physically faithful to her.

Staying true to your sacred vows of marriage is a badge of honor that you will be proud to wear openly for all to see. You should always strive to keep yourself morally strong.

When you keep your moral compass in check, you will be filled with pride that you are living the way that God wants you to live. Your inner self will feel great. Your spirits will be lifted. Your conscience will be clear. You will be more successful in all your endeavors because you are leading a Christian lifestyle, and you can do all things through Jesus Christ.

Your vows of marriage are a bond made until death do you part. That promise to your wife and to God is not meant to be broken. Just as you have faith in God's assurance of life ever after, so long as you believe in His Son, Jesus Christ, your wife has faith in you that you shall remain bonded to her, so long as you both shall live. If you expect God to keep His word to you, you should keep your word to Him since your marriage vows are a promise made with God's direction and approval.

Step 6
PUT YOUR WIFE BEFORE YOURSELF IN ALL THINGS

Do you treat your wife like a princess? Do you open her car door for her? Do you pull out her chair for her? Do you stand when she leaves the table? Do you listen to her point of view? Do you value her position and point of view as your wife?

When you met your wife, you probably went out of your way to show her how good your manners were and what a gentleman you were. How do you treat her now? In all truthfulness, you should be treating her even better than before.

If you were able to do the right things for your wife and demonstrate good manners during your courtship, those same manners should still be on display today. Don't let yourself fall into laziness and complacency in your marriage. Both traits are a personal weakness that need to be strengthened.

Men sometimes wonder why their wife isn't as amorous with them as they used to be. They wonder why the spark in their relationship has diminished. A marriage is a two-way street. Do you still hold your wife's hand? Do you put your arm around her? Are you happy to sit and have conversations about what's been going on in your lives?

Or do you just plop down in front of the TV, scroll through your cell phone, or head to the golf course? Do you make her the butt of your jokes or tease her about sensitive issues? Has doing your own thing while your wife does hers become a familiar pattern in your marriage?

If you put your wife first, you will find that the spark between the two of you remains bright because she feels you care about her and her wishes. It is easy to fall into a routine of doing the same thing day after day, which can result in a flat, lifeless relationship. Even though things may not change in your life for long periods of time, that doesn't mean that things need to become boring between you both.

When is the last time you read a new book or asked your wife what she's reading? You can't always demand that your spouse find something new and sparkling to add to your relationship. Make a concerted effort to investigate something new on your own or bring something new to your marriage by yourself. You could plan a spontaneous dinner at a new restaurant in town? It might not be your favorite type of food, but it's something different that the two of you can experience together. Even if it turns out to be the worst restaurant in the world, at least you tried to keep things interesting. Who knows? It might turn out to be a great restaurant with great food. Do new things with your wife on a continual basis. You will learn more about her every time, and she in turn will learn more about you.

Your life with your wife is a process of discovery. Think about what your wife likes and what your wife likes to do. Put her wishes first in your mind and try to do whatever you can to please her and surprise her. Take her to a chick flick. Even if you can't stand watching romantic, girly movies, you should make the effort to take her to a movie she wants to see.

She'll recognize you are trying to do something special and thoughtful for her. This alone will earn you great rewards as a loving Christian husband.

Your wife wants to feel special. She wants to feel like you are deeply in love with her and that she is the most important woman in the world to you. If she is, then treat her that way. Put her on your own pedestal and do all you can to let her know how much you love and appreciate her. It really doesn't take a lot of effort on your part. Even the smallest of things will register on your wife's radar, and she will be very appreciative of what you do for her.

In return, your wife will want to show you that she feels the same way about you and will make you feel like the most important man in the world to her.

"So they are no longer two, but one flesh. Therefore, what God has joined together, man must not separate" (Matthew 19:6 HCSB).

That's how a woman thinks. They have a great deal of reciprocity for returning favors that are given to them. Have you ever been invited to a friend's house for dinner? I'll bet you that as soon as you left their house, your wife was already asking when you might invite that same couple over for dinner at your house. That's the way the female brain operates. The more you give it, the more it wants to give back. Do all you can to give to your wife and to put her first in your life and she in turn will put you first in her life.

The loving feelings that you will begin to realize between you and your wife will be a direct result of what you give rather than what you receive.

"In every way I've shown you that by laboring like this, it is necessary to help the weak and to keep in mind the words of the Lord Jesus, for He said, 'It is more blessed to give than to receive'" (Acts 20:35 HCSB).

The rewards you will receive will astound you. But you have to give selflessly without thinking about personal gain, for the reward might not come as quickly as you'd hope (and may not even be what you'd expect). But, when you put your wife first, without any strings attached, you will be rewarded in due time, more than you could ever wish for.

Step 7
ESTABLISH LIFE GOALS WITH YOUR WIFE

Have you ever been on a long road trip or a cross-country drive? If you have, you know how important it is to plan the trip in advance before you go. Where are you headed? Where are you stopping along the way? How much money do you need to budget for gas, meals, and lodging?

Your marriage is like a lifelong road trip. Before you get married, you should have some frank discussions with your wife-to-be about certain life goals that will impact your relationship. Topics like religion, children, and finances must be up for discussion BEFORE you are married.

As you grow through marriage together with your wife, you'll encounter many detours that will require a change of course, but you need to make sure you both have similar destinations in mind for your life. Otherwise, you're in for a lot of unbearable confrontations and disastrous conflicts.

Imagine that you are deeply in love and have proposed to your wife-to-be. She accepts your proposal. Then you go to her parents' house and announce the great news, and your future mother-in-law bursts into tears of happiness because she will someday have grandchildren. What if you aren't sure you even want to have children? Things like that happen. Suddenly, you find yourself defending your choices about fatherhood before you are even married. This can cause a huge problem in your relationship.

How important is religion to you and your wife? Not everyone is raised in a religious family. There are many religions that frown on marriage between people of different faiths. Some religions even forbid such marriages unless the "outsider" converts to the religious belief system of the other.

"Do not be mismatched with unbelievers. For what partnership is there between righteousness and lawlessness? Or what fellowship does light have with darkness?" (2 Corinthians 6:14 HCSB).

You need to set life goals with your wife. No matter if you are newly engaged, newly married, or have been married a long time, it is never too late to establish life goals for you both to work toward together. If you don't set the goals together, you might have a different outlook on your future, and this will cause you to set individual goals that might send you in different directions.

Ideally, newlyweds should set a series of goals that are one year away, three years away, five years away, and ten years away. By setting these goals early in your relationship, you will have milestones that you can work toward accomplishing together, which will give you a shared future to invest in. As you reach these goals, you can then celebrate them together too.

Obviously, goals can change (and they certainly will to some degree). You might set a financial goal of saving $10,000 within three years. Just as you are getting close to your goal, you might face an unexpected job change or an emergency home improvement repair that causes you to spend most of your savings. Not reaching your financial goal should not be viewed as a failure, but rather, a successful solution to an unforeseen problem.

Adapting to change and resetting your plan accordingly still requires cooperation toward mutual goals. Concentrate on the positive. In the previous example, at least both of you had been saving money and were able to afford the unexpected expense. If you had not been saving money together and were spending all your excess income on expensive gifts to each other, you might not have been able to weather the storm.

Write down your life goals that you and your wife agree on and keep them somewhere prominent, so you'll be reminded of them often. Then work hard at trying to accomplish your ambitions as a couple. Your life goals are a plan, not a contract. Your plans can change for any number of reasons, and when they do, sit down with your wife and rework your life goals so that you are both on the same path together.

When my wife and I got married, I was the happiest man in the world and loved being married. After three years together, one day my wife had a doctor's appointment and he had asked her if she was ever going to have children, and if she was, she should do it soon since she was in her early thirties. That's all it took to convince my wife that it was time. As soon as she came home from her appointment, she said, "I'm ready to have a baby." Strangely enough, we had never had a serious discussion about having children. Thankfully, for us both, I have always loved children and knew that I wanted a family someday, so I was happy to pitch in and start having a family.

But what if I hadn't wanted children? This could have been a severe roadblock to our happy marriage and could have caused tremendous hardship for us both. I'm not blaming my parents for not instructing me about this, but it would have been nice to have some parental guidance about how to plan for marriage and children. I'm just guessing that my parents didn't receive the information from their parents, so they must have thought I'd just figure it out on my own when the time was right. Well, I did. And this is another reason I am writing this book: for the men in the world like me who didn't receive a blueprint on how to be a husband and a father. This book doesn't have every answer for every problem, but it will help you start to think and act differently, knowing that God is at your shoulder, proudly watching you become a loving Christian husband. God wants you to succeed. He created you to be one of His special children.

God blessed my wife and me with two great children, a boy and a girl, born two years apart, with my son born first. I often joke that "we ordered them right out of the Kmart catalog." Thank God we had the same family values and welcomed the opportunity to be parents.

Take time to inventory your life with your wife and set up life goals so that you will have a structured plan to pursue together. When you have a plan, it is easier to reach your goals.

When you have a plan, there won't be any last-minute surprises. You will both be working together in the same direction so that your marriage will be an overwhelming success.

"May he give you the desires of your heart and make all your plans succeed" (Psalm 20:4).

Step 8
TREASURE YOUR MARRIAGE AND YOUR WIFE

What is your pride and joy in life? Do you own a collector car? Do you have a favorite piece of artwork? Have you put together a collection of rare coins? What is it that you have that you are most proud of?

First should be your relationship with God, then your marriage with your wife, and then your children. Material things are simply items that have no real value in comparison to family. You could lose every one of your material possessions, and I'm sure you would be all right. But what if you lost your marriage or your children or your relationship with God? I'm sure it would have a devastating effect on you, both mentally and physically.

Your marriage is the first and best thing that you and your wife will have to build a life around. You should have the utmost pride in your marriage and in your wife so that nothing else in your physical world will ever be more important.

I say physical world because you and your wife should share a love for God that is the highest priority in your spiritual world. God should be the trophy you display on your personal mantle and are proud to share with anyone you meet.

God wants you to have a loving marriage and a loving wife. That is why He created man and woman so that they would be a perfect couple to venture through life together. Realize that God has blessed you with a loving wife and that you should love and respect God's choice for you.

When you show respect for your marriage and wife before the rest of the world, you are honoring God's blessings for you. The joy and happiness you will get from respecting your wife and marriage will be a foundation that will support your relationship throughout all times, both good and bad.

There will be plenty of difficulties in your marriage, but your respect for your wife and your marriage will help you weather the difficulties that arise. You might suffer a miscarriage in a pregnancy. You might have financial difficulties. You might lose your home to a tornado, wildfire, or other natural disaster. The possibilities are endless.

But, when you respect your marriage and your wife, you will realize that the two of you together, with a shared faith in God's love, can weather any situation that may come your way.

"And if someone overpowers one person, two can resist him. A cord of three strands is not easily broken" (Ecclesiastes 4:12 CSB).

If, on the other hand, you do not respect your marriage and your wife, you will cause a crack in the foundation of your marriage that will continue to widen and separate until you and your wife are on opposite sides of the problem. Without your combined strength as a married couple, you will be forced to attack your problems alone, thereby causing your wife to face her problems alone too. This is a sure-fire way to erode the bond of love and respect that God has intended for you both.

When you do not respect your marriage and your wife, you are denying God's plans for you. Since God has the ability to know the number of every hair on your head, He will have a plan for you and your wife, and by not respecting God's plan, you are denying God's love for you. Acknowledge God and His Son Jesus Christ, your Lord and Savior.

"Indeed, the hairs of your head are all counted. Don't be afraid; you are worth more than many sparrows! And I say to you, anyone who acknowledges Me before men, the Son of Man will also acknowledge him before the angels of God, but whoever denies Me before men will be denied before the angels of God" (Luke 12:7–9 HCSB).

Step 9
BE THE CHRISTIAN LEADER OF YOUR HOME

A leader has many traits at his disposal to draw upon that allow him to find peaceful solutions for the most difficult problems. Make no mistake about it, even if you become a loving Christian husband, you will still be faced with difficult problems in your marriage from time to time. They might not always be personal conflicts with your wife—the problems could be financial, they could be medical, they could be with a neighbor, or they could be with other relatives. The list is endless.

As a Christian leader, you must learn how to discover the humble, loving person deep inside your heart and let that part of you be your guiding light in the world. Your wife needs to know that your actions are not temporary but rather are a part of your moral fiber and your day-to-day way of life. She needs to know that you are grounded in your approach to problem-solving and that no matter what the problem is, you will have a level-headed approach to locating a solution based on your moral and spiritual beliefs. Solving a problem doesn't mean that you will always get your way—it means that you have identified the problem, gathered the necessary facts, and developed a solution that ultimately pleases

God. When you do things with an effort to make God happy, you will always reach the best solution possible. If God is happy with your decision, how can mortal man be any less satisfied?

With all of the macho attitudes and posturing shown on social media and movies nowadays, men have become more confrontational in our world and more easily angered and offended. Being surrounded by this behavior makes it even more difficult to try and rise above the fray to take the right path that a Christian leader should follow.

God planted a loving heart deep inside of you that contains compassion, sympathy, understanding, nurturing, and genuine affection for your wife, children, and every living person and thing. God wants you to fulfill His wishes of having love for all others. How is it possible for you to love every living person when we encounter so many difficult people on a daily basis? Angry drivers, rude waiters, aggressive panhandlers? It's difficult to overcome our stereotypes and prejudices when we meet a stranger for the first time, causing us to avoid loving our neighbors as ourselves. The evil of the world has made each of us more wary of strangers (and justifiably so), which makes it easier for us to convince ourselves to just not get involved.

But as we know from the Bible, a teacher of the law approached Jesus and His disciples and asked:

"Teacher, which is the greatest commandment in the Law?" Jesus replied: "'Love the Lord your God with all your heart and with all your soul and with all your mind.' This is the first and greatest commandment. And the second is like it: 'Love your neighbor as yourself.' All the Law and the Prophets hang on these two commandments" (Matthew 22:36–40 NIV).

Therefore, you should love your neighbor as yourself and wake up every day asking that God use you to be of help to somebody else in need. The word *neighbor* is not restricted to the person living next door to you. I believe the word *neighbor* is meant to cover any person other than yourself, as all of God's children are created equal. God used the same amount of love to create you that He used to create me. Therefore, are we not all brothers and sisters equal in God's love? Shouldn't we love and respect each other based on that simple fact alone?

This means that you should have a genuine love for everyone at all times. Knowing that God has placed this mandate in your heart, it is up to you to follow that instruction so that you are performing God's will in your life. God wants you to love and help others.

Especially in their times of need.

When you begin to look for people in need, you will suddenly discover they are all around you. Some will have small needs; others will have enormous needs. Some needs are emotional, others are physical or financial. For instance, you can help a child tie a shoe, open the door for someone, help a person put their walker into the trunk of their car, return someone else's shopping cart for them—there's never a bad moment when you give of your time to a stranger in need. Not only will you make them feel better, but you'll also make yourself feel better in the process. And you will please God by doing what He intended for you to do.

You can give in many ways other than just financial support. You might have a special talent as a handyman, coach, electrician, teacher, plumber, gardener, painter, mechanic, or accountant that will allow you to help others who might be in need. This doesn't mean that you have to volunteer to paint an entire house inside and out, but you should pitch in freely and offer to help others whenever you can by being a Christian leader.

Accept the personal challenge of being the Christian leader of your home, and you will reap the benefits of making the world a better place every time you extend a hand to others.

One day, I was driving down the street a mile or so from my house and noticed that a large tree had fallen on a fence in front of the home of someone I didn't know. My first thought was that I was glad it didn't happen at my house. I also thought that person would cut up the tree for firewood, so I just passed by without stopping. However, after several weeks, I noticed the fallen tree was still in the same place and that the broken fence was allowing the homeowner's horses to escape the yard and graze near the side of the road. So, I decided to stop and see if I might help cut the tree and mend the fence. After all, what man doesn't love to use a chainsaw?

I knocked on the "neighbor's" door, and after a few moments, I heard some shuffling footsteps on the other side. I introduced myself to the older gentleman who lived there and asked if he might need some help with the tree. He said he had recently had a stroke and wasn't able to cut the tree himself. He also said he was on a fixed income and didn't have much money, but he asked how much I would charge him for cutting the tree the rest of the way down. I told him I was a neighbor from further down the street and that I didn't want any money, but that I just felt like God had asked me to stop and offer some help. He was pretty emotional as he gladly accepted my assistance. It took me a couple of days to cut the tree, split the logs into firewood, and mend his fence so his horses wouldn't get out. But those few hours invested in helping a neighbor was time well spent as I saw the joy on his face once the job was completed. No amount of money could have bought me the happiness I felt inside by being able to help a neighbor in need.

On another day, I was walking across the parking lot at work and saw a fellow coworker walking my way. I recognized her from another department, but I had never spoken to her and didn't even really know her name. As we passed each other, our eyes briefly locked, and I noticed that her eyes were full of tears. I could have just let her go, but something deep in my heart took over and I asked if she was all right.

She paused, not sure whether to look my way, and I asked again if she was okay. When she turned my way, I could barely hear her words as she told me she had just learned that her younger brother had suddenly passed away that morning.

Even though we were two strangers, I wrapped her in my arms and held her as she sobbed. As she continued to cry and bury her head on my shoulder, I just started saying a prayer to God to have mercy on her brother's soul. Her sobs slowly quieted down as she regained her composure, and then she thanked me with a small smile. I know that God placed me in her path to provide a brief escape from the pain she was feeling.

God didn't place us on this earth to simply stay in our own little world and ignore everything around us. We have all been created according to God's will so that we can help each other, and by doing so, we help ourselves.

Sometimes we fall short in God's eyes by doing things we shouldn't do. On the other hand, we also fall short in His eyes by NOT doing things that we should do.

As you start to help others who cross your path, you'll not only become more observant of your surroundings, but you'll also be happier deep inside your heart almost all the time. When you're happy deep inside, the outside world does not affect you the same as it does when you aren't so happy inside. Don't ever be too busy with your own life to try and help someone else with their life.

The fact that you are being the Christian leader of your house will set a good example for your wife, your children, and others in your neighborhood and community.

When you are the Christian leader of your house, others will notice without you having to say anything about it. Your attitude will change, your behavior will change, your demeanor will change, and you will begin to discover that you have an inner peace that makes your life more enjoyable—not only for you but also for others around you.

Your role as a Christian leader of your home does not mean that you should only act that way within the four walls of your own house. As the Christian leader of your home, it is up to you to set the example for others in your family. Your actions (or inactions) will set the tone of what sort of household you develop for your family. When your wife sees that you accept your role as a Christian husband and leader, she will gain confidence in your ability to navigate the perils of life, and she will feel comfortable going through life as your loving Christian wife.

By being a strong Christian leader as a husband, that foundation will allow your wife to grow closer to you and form a bond that is unbreakable. She will have confidence in your ability to deal with problems as she witnesses the way you reach into your inner heart and treat others around you with the same love you have for yourself and for Jesus Christ.

Over time, your Christian attitude of leading your household will allow you to feel closer to God and His Son Jesus Christ by knowing that your goals are pleasing to God and all those around you.

Step 10
ALWAYS TREAT YOUR MARRIAGE LIKE A WORK IN PROGRESS

You are the luckiest man in the world if you are fortunate enough to find a Christian lady as your wife whom you can love, cherish, honor, and protect for all the days of your life.

It's not easy to build a strong Christian marriage. It requires steadfast, intentional commitment every day. But the rewards you will reap by accepting the challenge will benefit you forever. When you have a strong Christian marriage, you will never be alone, for your wife will be at your side each day. You will understand how important your wife is to you and the blessing God gave to you by finding a Christian lady to marry.

I remember to this day the feeling I had as my bride walked through the church doors in her wedding dress. She was the most beautiful woman in the world, and she was walking down the aisle to join me in marriage with God as my witness. Tears came to my eyes as I soaked up the vision of her dressed in white, and I felt like the proudest man ever.

I still feel that way. You should too. You should do everything you can to let your wife know each and every day how happy you are with her. I know that sounds impossible because everyone has faults, arguments, and differences, but you have to be able to look past all of those things and focus on the most important fact of all: your wife chose you to be her husband forever.

Marriage isn't a trial run. Most people honestly believe that they are getting married for the rest of their life, and I pray that's the way it is with you and your wife. If you loved your wife enough to marry her in the first place, then you should do everything you can to sustain that commitment and build your relationship so strong that nothing can ever take it apart. If you do all you can to make your wife feel that she made a great choice in having you as a husband, your marriage will last until death do you part.

Establishing a strong, loving Christian relationship that builds on itself is the best thing you will ever do. Having children with your wife will be the next best thing you will ever do. Raising your children as a loving Christian father is the next best thing after that. (See the next section of this book, *10 Steps to Being a Loving Christian Father.*)

"Grandchildren are the crown of the elderly, and the pride of children is their fathers" (Proverbs 17:6 CSB).

"Sons are indeed a heritage from the LORD, offspring, a reward. Like arrows in the hand of a warrior are the sons born in one's youth. Happy is the man who has filled his quiver with them. Such men will never be put to shame when they speak with their enemies at the city gate" (Psalm 127:3–5 CSB).

You should try your hardest every day to strengthen your marriage. Bring your wife flowers. Give her compliments. Don't be fussy about things. Help her whenever you can. Do fun things together.

Never go to bed mad at each other. Work out your problems in private. Don't embarrass your wife in front of others. Don't talk badly about your wife to anyone else. Show her love and affection every day. Leave her love notes around the house. Write her a love poem.

I know these things sound mushy, but if you neglect to do small, special things for your wife, you are neglecting your relationship. Just like a new car needs regular maintenance to keep it running at peak performance, your wife and your marriage need regular maintenance to help keep your love burning brightly.

Don't just accept the fact that you are married forever and only go through the basic motions every day. Remember that your wife is a blessing given to you by God and that it is your responsibility to cherish that blessing forever. When you understand how important your marriage is to your success as a husband and father, you will honor and value your marriage with love and respect so that you are proud of what you have.

The prouder you are of your marriage, the more your love will blossom for your wife and the stronger her love will grow for you. This loving partnership sanctioned by God is a living, breathing union of two unique human beings who have been joined together for all of eternity.

You are your wife's Adam, and she is your Eve. God made you especially for each other to be husband and wife, to bear children together, and to carry on His plan for the world. Dedicate yourself to being a loving Christian husband. Accept the challenge God has placed in front of you and make every day better than the day before.

"Then the LORD God said, 'It is not good for the man to be alone.

I will make a helper as his complement'" (Genesis 2:18 HCSB).

By following God's path for you and your wife, you will have a strong Christian marriage that is built on a foundation of love and respect, which will give you great rewards forever and ever.

As you follow that path, you will find that you need to always take care of your own business by doing what is right for a man to do. You will need to carry your part of the marriage vows by stepping up and trying your hardest to keep the love flame alive inside of you. You will have to adopt the belief that it is your responsibility to do the right thing all the time. Just as you understand that your body breathes on its own without you having to tell it to breathe, you will also need to develop the ability to live life as a strong Christian man without having to think about it. It needs to be woven into your daily way of life and become a part of who you are as a loving Christian husband.

You can't let your love go untended, or you will find your relationship headed toward boredom. Just as you need fresh oxygen in order to keep living, you need to pay close attention to your wife, to keep flirting with her, and to provide fresh love in order to keep your relationship alive and strong.

Why should you have to flirt? After all, you're already married.

The reason you flirt with your wife is to keep a spark of excitement glowing underneath your marriage. The glowing embers will spark the flames that build into a bonfire of love, so long as you always keep trying to improve your relationship.

You can't just get married and believe that things will be perfect for the rest of your life. Working to improve your relationship is a valuable tool that ensures your marriage will grow stronger and last through the difficult times that are sure to arise.

As with any project (and yes, marriage is a project), you need to be able to examine your progress and adapt as necessary to handle any changes that might present themselves. No matter how difficult the challenge to your marriage might seem, if you have a strong bond that you work at improving, you will be able to weather any storm, especially with God's help.

"No temptation has overtaken you except what is common to mankind. And God is faithful; he will not let you be tempted beyond what you can bear. But when you are tempted, he will also provide a way out so that you can endure it" (1 Corinthians 10:13 NIV).

The way out of a temptation will not always be directly in front of you, nor will it be easily found. God wants you to develop the ability to look at your situation from all angles so that you are able to discover the way out on your own. Oftentimes through a very painful awakening or self-realization. But there is always a solution available to those who look hard enough.

This is especially true in your relationship with your wife. As you nurture your marriage, you will be adapting to the elements of change that are ever-present throughout your life. Do not think that once you say, "I do," the rest of your marriage will be a bowl of cherries. As you and your wife grow older together, the changes you both experience will shift the direction of your lives along many paths, and it is important for you to enjoy the journey of change with someone you love and cherish.

Your marriage will be like planting a tree. When a young tree is newly planted, it can easily be propped up and supported so that it grows straight and tall. Small changes in the direction of the tree's growth can be countered with very minimal force. However, as the tree grows larger and has been in the ground longer, changing the direction of growth becomes more difficult and even impossible. That is why it is so important to always keep paying attention to your marriage and to make the small changes necessary along the way so that the marriage continues to grow tall and strong. Do not allow your marriage to grow crooked or bent, or else you will one day discover that it is virtually impossible to correct the direction.

In essence, your role as a loving Christian husband is to remain observant of your marriage and your behavior so that your path ultimately leads to pleasing God.

Your time on earth is a split-second compared to the vastness of your eternal life. To make sure your life is abundant and joyful, you should strive to be positive, loving, caring, helpful, and thankful for everything with which you are blessed. Value the blessings that God has granted to you and do not squander the opportunities that you have been given. Protect your family, love your family, and provide the Christian leadership that they need so that your household reflects God's love.

There is no greater satisfaction in this life than knowing you are doing things that will please God. When you think of the creative miracles that God provided so that you became a human being, you will understand that He created you out of love and that He will love you unconditionally all the days of your life, throughout eternity. In return, once you understand this love, you will also understand that the only way to repay God for His love is to offer your love in return: love to yourself, love to your wife, love to your children, love to your neighbors, love to Jesus Christ, and love to Lord God Almighty.

The Bible tells us in Genesis that God took seven days to create all things. It was not accomplished in one single day. God has shown us from the beginning that things take time to complete and that there is a nurturing process required to achieve the finished product.

Therefore, continue to nurture your marriage and your love for your wife so that you make it your goal to live a Christian life of love for everyone and everything around you.

When you discover the joy of being a loving Christian husband, you will ultimately be rewarded for your efforts by having a Christian wife who will love and support you throughout all your days. Having a loving, supportive wife will make the journey of life the most enjoyable experience you could ever ask for. Continue to hold up your end of the deal by being a Christian husband, and in return, you will receive God's reward of having a blessed, Christian marriage.

Value your role as a Christian man and understand that God has created you to nurture mankind for future generations. Do your part to assist God's plans so that your works are pleasing to Him, and you will be able to pass happily into heaven knowing that you walked throughout your earthly days with God as your guide and Jesus Christ as your Lord and Savior.

Having accomplished that, you will succeed at being a loving Christian Husband.

"10 Steps to Being a Loving Christian Father"

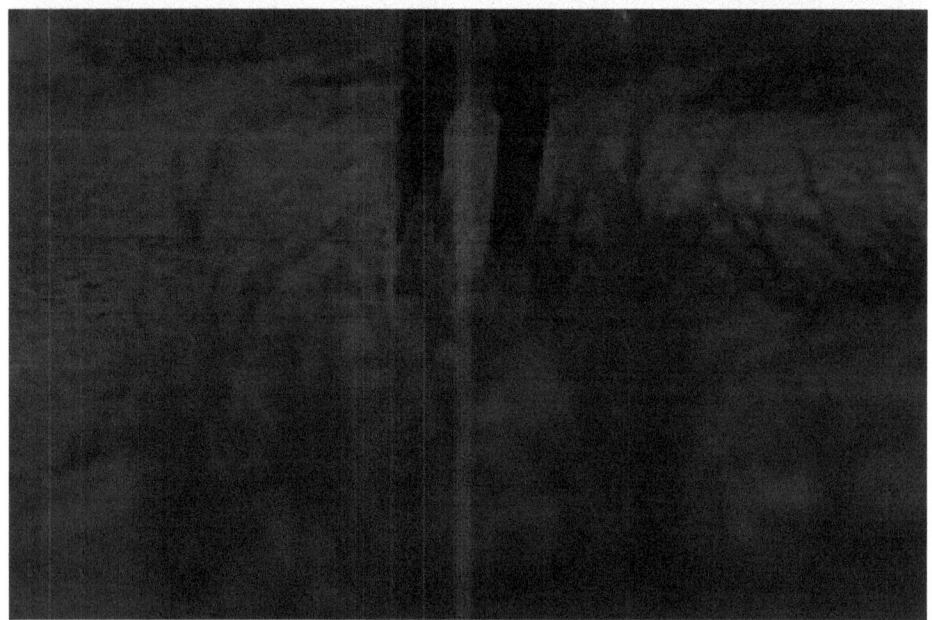

INTRODUCTION
To Being a Loving Christian Father

Every day there are numerous reports of young people falling prey to sin, prison, and sometimes even death because of their self-destructive paths. One thing most of these tragic stories have in common is the lack of a strong father figure—more to the point, the lack of a loving Christian father.

My heart hurts when I see the negative results everywhere around me—underage smoking, underage drinking, bullying, suicide, drug abuse, unwed pregnancies, profanity, juvenile crime, gangs, graffiti, teenage runaways. The list goes on and on.

It's not just the fault of the child. I believe a lot of the fault falls on the shoulders of the person who fathered that child—a father who neglects his duties as spelled out in the Bible:

"Fathers, do not provoke your children to anger, but bring them up in the discipline and instruction of the Lord" (Ephesians 6:4 ESV).

It is the mandate of God that it is a man's responsibility and duty as a father to show his children the right way to live, the proper way to behave, and the righteous way to grow up. It is a father's actions or inactions that help dictate the path of success for his children. Much like a lighthouse that prevents a ship from crashing into the rocky shoreline, a loving father should also be a guiding beacon for their child drifting through treacherous waters.

Placing all the responsibility on a father might seem unfair since a child ultimately makes their own choices in life. But I personally believe a child's behavior is directly influenced by the father figure (or lack of a father figure) in their life.

Yes, the child has a mother too, and while the mother has a significant and equally important role in raising the child, there is no substitute in a child's life for a loving Christian father. The same is true that there is no substitute for a loving Christian mother.

That is why God made it necessary for there to be a man and woman together in order to make a child. That is the God-given way.

"So God created man in His own image; He created him in the image of God; He created them male and female" (Genesis 1:27 HCSB).

God created man and woman to "be fruitful, and multiply" (Genesis 1:28 KJV) and then work together as a couple to provide their children with the support and instruction that are unique to each parent. A man will be able to provide things to a child that only a man can provide, and a woman can provide things that only a woman can provide.

"This is why a man leaves his father and mother and bonds with his wife, and they become one flesh" (Genesis 2:24 CSB).

It is important to notice in this passage that "father" is mentioned first as God created man first. The father is the strength of the family and is supported in child-rearing by the wife, who is equally important. This book is meant to help guide you in your role as a Christian father and is not meant to diminish the role of the mother.

Unfortunately, many men go through life without any direction or advice about how to build and nurture a family successfully, especially if they had a father figure who did not offer them the proper love or guidance that they needed in their own upbringing.

But even growing up with excellent male role models doesn't necessarily make a man immune to personal shortcomings as a father.

Being a good father isn't easy, but the rewards are great. This book is intended to help guide you along the path to becoming a loving Christian father to your children so that you may receive the paternal rewards of being an excellent dad.

"The father of the righteous will greatly rejoice; he who fathers a wise son will be glad in him" (Proverbs 23:24 ESV).

In my opinion, the father has the ultimate responsibility to raise a child the right way in a loving Christian home. The father is the head of the household. That doesn't mean that he must be a tyrannical leader without compassion or understanding, or that he does not need to listen to input from his wife, but it does mean that you, as a father, are obligated to assume the role of spiritual leader in your household and become a loving Christian father to your children.

Lacking the skills to do so does not make you a bad father. That simply means that unless someone showed you the right way as you were growing up, it's difficult to find the solutions all by yourself. And if you are anything like me, you were raised by a father who worked hard to support his family but offered little guidance about having and raising children, so the routine perpetuates itself over and over, generation after generation.

It is difficult enough just to earn a living, pay the bills, raise the kids, and be a good husband. We fathers spend so many of our hours each day just trying to keep on top of things that there's virtually no time left to look at ourselves and see how we can improve our role as a father.

This book was written to give you a series of practical steps to follow so that you can raise your child with love, respect, and care. In doing so, you will build a relationship with your child that will allow you and your family to reap the benefits of your role as a loving Christian father. There's not a better feeling in the world as a father than when your child wraps their arms around your neck and whispers, "I love you, Daddy."

Also, there's not a better feeling in the world for a child than to be wrapped up in their father's arms and told "I love you too."

Being a great father doesn't just mean that you're protective of your child and telling a big story of all you do for your family to your friends. Being a great father is to understand the role you will be playing in raising your "flower" to help it bloom as beautifully as possible. You will be watering that flower, giving it nutrients, protecting it from seasonal changes, keeping the weeds away, and even pruning stems and branches that might inhibit its growth.

God will provide the sunshine.

No matter what age your children are or if you're just beginning your fatherhood journey, this book will give you helpful guidelines to follow to help you raise your child with respect, love, and an emphasis on a Christian upbringing. As your child feels the comfort of your love and care, they will reciprocate those same feelings and form a parental bond of trust with you. The foundation for their future success is built slowly, day by day, and you will become a huge blessing in your child's life when you provide the proper guidance and advice.

While these steps will take time to incorporate into your daily life, you will start to see immediate changes in your relationship with your child as soon as you begin to implement them. At first, you will have to make a conscious effort to practice these steps, but soon they will become a way of living that's easily applied in your everyday routine. You will find them enjoyable to utilize, and the results will be life-changing for you and your family. I believe that you will enjoy seeing your relationship improve with your children, and you will feel a glow of satisfaction knowing that you are doing God's will in raising your children in His favor.

The secret of these ten steps is that they do not require you to instruct your child how to change and behave, but rather, they ask you to examine and strengthen your own actions. By altering your approach, you will be showing and telling your child how much you care for them, and they will understand your words and actions without any prompting.

This book is about how to help you become a loving Christian father. Maybe you are already? But, if you follow these steps and strive to be the best Christian father you can be, your children will love and respect you for it and will gladly follow in your path. The man who strives to become a great Christian father will receive many untold blessings in his life and will pass along great Christian children as an inheritance to the world. That alone will make you a success and give you the comfort of knowing that you honored God with your actions.

Good luck with your life and may God bless you for wanting to improve your relationship with your children as a loving Christian Father.

Step 1
ASK GOD FOR HELP

Men are the stronger sex. Men carry the heavy loads. Men are made to work hard. Men do the dirty work. Men suck it up and just keep going.

These adages of strength and masculinity have been instilled in man since the beginning of time. When God created Adam on the sixth day, God knew that Adam was both lonely and overwhelmed with the world around him and that he needed companionship and help.

"The Lord God said, 'It is not good for the man to be alone. I will make a helper suitable for him" (Genesis 2:18 NIV).

The suitable helper God made for man was woman. God does not want you to be alone in the world to carry the heavy burdens of life by yourself. He wants you to share your burden with a suitable mate. He wants you to have a loving Christian wife and produce loving Christian children.

"For this reason, a man will leave his father and mother and be united to his wife, and they will become one flesh" (Genesis 2:24 NIV).

You, however, as a loving Christian father, are to be the strength of your family, to raise your children as God has planned. Do not shirk your duties as a father and think that other family members should raise your child. It is your responsibility alone to be the father.

If you are man enough to make a child, you are man enough to become a loving Christian father and make the sacrifices necessary to raise your child the right way.

God wants you to have help in all that you do. That is why He made woman as a suitable partner. To be a loving Christian father, you must also be a loving Christian husband to raise your child in a loving Christian home.

God has made it possible for you to be a loving Christian father by giving you the choice to have a wife as a helper in the journey of life. Accept your wife's help openly and warmly. Make your marriage a strong partnership that is built to withstand the multitude of worldly trials and tribulations that will come your way.

You can learn about building a strong marriage in the first section of this book *10 Steps to Being a Loving Christian Husband.*

Even if your relationship with your wife needs nurturing, you must still do all you can to give your child a Christian upbringing so that they will do the same for their children. Then, future generations of your family lineage will have a legacy and a foundation to build on.

A rock-solid foundation.

Even if you were not raised by a loving Christian father, you must be the one to plant the first seed of faith for it to multiply in future generations. Be the one that starts the tradition for your descendants to follow, and you will become great in their memories, for you are leading them to the promise of Christian living, salvation, and resurrection.

Despite His gift of a wife as a helpmate, God still expects you to ask Him for additional help through prayer. Do not assume He wants you to be tough and go through the struggles of life without His divine guidance. God wants to know that you can ask for His help. If you are vain enough to think that you can maneuver through this life without His help, you will miss the opportunity of a loving relationship with God.

"Which of you fathers, if your son asks for a fish, will give him a snake instead? Or if he asks for an egg, will give him a scorpion?

If you then, though you are evil, know how to give good gifts to your children, how much more will your Father in heaven give the Holy Spirit to those who ask him!" (Luke 11:11–13 NIV).

Have you ever undertaken a huge task on your own that is so overwhelming that it seems impossible to complete? Maybe you were laying pallets of sod in your yard? Maybe you were removing junk and debris from a relative's house? Maybe you were helping neighbors recover from a tornado or other disaster? Sure, you can do it by yourself, but think about how difficult that task is when you are by yourself. Now think about how you feel when someone steps in to help.

The sudden feeling of relief and friendship that arises inside of you suddenly makes the job easier. It makes the task at hand move more quickly. The isolated, lonely struggle you were facing is now a joint venture that is easier to shoulder and more enjoyable as you share the struggle with your friends and neighbors.

God wants to share your struggles with you. He wants you to ask for His help. He wants to feel important in your life. He wants to know that you realize that things in life are easier when He is invited to help.

Don't be so manly that you are afraid to ask for His help. Don't worry about how it will be done. Just trust in your faith. God loves to give his help to anyone who asks.

"Do not be anxious about anything, but in every situation, by prayer and petition, and with thanksgiving, present your requests to God. And the peace of God, which transcends all understanding, will guard your hearts and your minds in Christ Jesus" (Philippians 4:6–7 NIV).

It is okay to ask for things in your prayers. Develop a ritual time to pray. Pray more than once a day. Pray in the morning when you first awaken. Pray at meals. Pray before bedtime. Pray openly with your children so that they know you have a personal relationship and belief in God. When your children hear you praying on their behalf, they will understand how much you love them, and in turn, they will feel safe and secure under your guidance. When your child feels safe and secure, they will be respectful and reverent to you since they know that you are their protector and that you are walking with God on your side.

They will trust you and they will love you.

When you pray, ask God for help in your daily struggles. Count your blessings. Be appreciative of the great wife and great children that God has given you. Give special thanks for God's sacrifice of his only Son, Jesus Christ, who died on the cross to save you from your sins. Ask for mercy and guidance throughout the day to help you follow God's will. Ask for safety for your family and for your loved ones to remain free of sickness and injury. Ask for forgiveness of your sins and for those who may sin against you. Give thanks for the ability to build a relationship with God through the prayers you offer.

Ask for God's help in all that you do, and you will be richly rewarded by His mercy and love. You will begin to feel an inner strength when you know that you are following God's will. You will feel confident that you are walking down the righteous path that makes God happy, and you will notice a change in your attitude, your personality, and your relationships with your wife and children. And they will notice the change in you too.

Do not be bashful about leading prayers for your family or friends. You are the father of the family and the host of your home. You set the standards that your family will follow. If you don't offer family prayers at meals or other times, how will your children learn? Do not be embarrassed to put your arms around your family and ask them to join you in giving thanks to God for what He has provided to you. Your children are a miracle blessing that has been given to you by God's mercy and grace, and He expects you to take care of those blessings with all your heart and all of your strength and all of your mind and all of your soul.

A family that prays together stays together.

Ask God for His help and He will provide, just as Jesus assures us in Matthew 6:31-34:

"So don't worry, saying, 'What will we eat?' or 'What will we drink?' or 'What will we wear?' For the Gentiles eagerly seek all these things, and your heavenly Father knows that you need them. But seek first the kingdom of God and his righteousness, and all these things will be provided for you. Therefore, don't worry about tomorrow, because tomorrow will worry about itself. Each day has enough trouble of its own" (CSB).

Step 2
BE THANKFUL FOR WHAT GOD HAS BLESSED YOU WITH

Count your blessings every day. Don't take for granted that which God has given to you and do not rush for final results. Instead, enjoy the journey to its fullest.

"A faithful person will have many blessings, but one in a hurry to get rich will not go unpunished" (Proverbs 20:28 CSB).

If you are blessed enough to have a child, you are the luckiest man in the world. Even during those trying times of the toddler years or terrible twos when your little bundle of joy is acting like a demon-possessed rug rat, you should realize the miracle of life and how fortunate you are to have fathered a child.

Some of life's most memorable moments of being a father happen during those volatile times when the world seems to be falling apart—for instance, when your child throws a temper tantrum in the middle of the toy aisle at Walmart. No matter how angelic you might believe your child to be, they all have at least one meltdown in the toy department at some point. It's how you deal with that meltdown that shows your true character as a loving Christian father. While it might seem like a huge burden or a scary future, understand that your child also has one of the luckiest advantages in the world in that YOU are their father.

Once you understand the miracle of life and the huge responsibility that goes with being a father, you will cherish the role of being a loving Christian father. You will also accept the challenge of raising a wonderful child who will carry your values forward into future generations.

From the moment you first discover you are going to be a father; your life will be changed forever.

No matter what the circumstances of your pregnancy are, embrace the experience and give thanks to God for the gift of life that is coming your way. There are countless numbers of men in this world who will never have the joy of being a father. There are countless numbers of children in the world who will never know the joy of having a father, so give your child the special gift that only you can give.

Make it your personal quest to be a loving Christian father and accept the responsibility it brings.

Not only is your child special—you are special as well. God has selected you to bear the enormous challenge of raising a child that will carry on your bloodline for future generations.

When you understand that the child you are going to have is a gift from God, you will understand how important it is to take care of that special gift and to protect it with every ounce of your body. Knowing that your child is created from your body will make you realize the huge responsibility you have to nurture and love that child beyond all boundaries.

Rejoice in the opportunity to be a loving Christian father. You have the chance to help make the world a better place by raising your child with love and affection so that they become a positive influence on society. Only God knows the future path of your children, and you must do all you can to ensure God's plan is treated with respect and dignity so that your child will allow God's will to be done in their own lives.

Be eager to play a guiding role in your child's life. From the first moment you hear the heartbeat of your unborn child, you should begin to feel the surge of pride inside your own body, knowing that you are among God's chosen people to be a loving Christian father. You created that heartbeat through God's will, and He has granted an experience to you like no other.

When you see the ultrasound of your tiny baby curled inside of your wife's womb, you will begin to witness God's miracle of life forming right before your very eyes. What started as a microscopic seed from inside your body soon becomes a biological miracle as the human cells reproduce and regenerate by the billions, forming fingers, toes, eyes, lungs, a heart, a brain, and every other vital organ.

It is beyond all comprehension how each of those cells knows how to grow into brain cells, heart cells, lung cells, blood cells, and every organ necessary to sustain the life that God created with His hands from the very beginning of time. To those unbelievers in the world who think that life is merely an accidental result of two huge rocks colliding in outer space, they are oblivious to explain the fact that there are trillions upon trillions of miracles that surround us each and every day that could only have been placed there through the creative genius of our God. Just imagine how many things are happening to your child as they grow through the gestation period inside the womb of their mother.

In your prayers, give thanks to God for the gift of a child. You will develop a strong love and affection for your child that is the foundation of being a loving Christian father. And after strengthening that bond, you will come to another realization that will tear your heart out. The overwhelming understanding of the sacrifice God made for you when He sent His Son, Jesus Christ, to die on the cross for your sins.

"For God so loved the world that he gave his one and only Son, that whoever believes in Him shall not perish but have eternal life" (John 3:16 NIV).

What a great promise this is from God to you. Think about this for a moment. *God, who is a father like I am, allowed His one and only Son to die on the cross for me and for all other sinners of the world.*

Put yourself in God's place for just a moment and think about sacrificing your own child for the sinners of the world. For people you don't even know. Sacrifice is too pretty of a word for what God did with His one and only Son. Here's what He did for you. For all of us.

God allowed Jesus to be betrayed by someone close to Him who was filled with Satan. God allowed Jesus to be ridiculed and marched along a street of jeering, taunting tormentors, carrying a heavy wooden cross on his shoulders. God allowed His own Son to be nailed to that cross and hang there in agony until He breathed His last breath. Can you imagine the pain you would feel as a father as you watch your child have heavy spikes hammered through their hands and feet? The same tiny hands and feet you held in your own arms when your child was a newborn.

And God watched from heaven as Jesus Christ was raised on a cross, wearing a crown of sharp thorns that punctured his skin and sent blood cascading down his face. He watched as Jesus Christ died slowly and painfully on the cross between two ordinary criminals. Even then, Jesus asked for the forgiveness of those who had persecuted Him.

"When they arrived at the place called The Skull, they crucified him there, along with the criminals, one on the right and one on the left. Then Jesus said, 'Father, forgive them, because they do not know what they are doing.'" (Luke 23:33–34 CSB).

God had to have cried that day, just as you would have, had it been your own child that you willingly sacrificed.

When you understand how much God loves you since He gave His one and only Son to die for your sins, you will have a new awakening in

God's love for you as you contemplate the thought of never having to sacrifice your own child as their sins were forgiven by the blood of Jesus Christ.

Be thankful for the child that God has gifted into your life and love that child the same as God loves you. Let your child know that you love them and be thankful every day for having your child in your life.

Your child will feel true love coming from you and will always welcome the warmth and safety of the relationship you will build through the love that you have for each other.

A loving Christian father loves his children forever, no matter what. Just as God loves each of you, no matter what you have done.

So long as you ask for forgiveness and leave your sins behind you, you will have an eternal home in heaven with God and His Son Jesus Christ.

Give thanks every day for the blessing God has given you as witnessed by His sending you a child to care for.

Step 3
OPENLY SHARE YOUR LOVE WITH YOUR CHILD

Men are thinkers and planners. Men contemplate things in life. Men are more about action than words. Some people talk the talk, but real men walk the walk.

How many times have we heard these things said about the way men operate in life? Of the ten steps in this book, one of the hardest might be opening your love up so it is visible to your child and to others.

You might have a heart of gold and love your child more than anything in this world—but do you tell your child how you feel? Do you show them? I don't mean by buying them gifts and getting them the latest designer goodies. I mean, do you really show them how much you love them with your actions and your words?

The most important thing you can do to openly share your love with your child is to have a direct one-on-one talk with them that lets them know exactly how you feel about them.

Choose a special place to have your talk. Don't do it at home in the kitchen or in the car. These are your usual fields of encounter and already have too many other memories associated with them.

Perhaps there were even heated arguments in some of these places at another time? I challenge you to find a special place where your child has never been before to share your special message of love.

Find a "fairy-tale" setting such as a museum, a bench in a beautiful park, a horse-drawn carriage, an ice cream parlor, bleachers at a local ballpark, or anywhere neutral that your child will remember fondly. It might not seem important to you, but to a child, being in a storybook setting can make your heart-to-heart talk unforgettable.

Don't tell your child, "Hey, let's go somewhere and have a heart-to-heart talk." This will immediately put them on guard, and they'll wonder what they did wrong. Just say something simple like,

"Hey, I found something neat I want to share with you. Come on.

Let's go for a ride."

It doesn't matter what age your child is for you to have this special moment with them. Obviously, babies and toddlers aren't going to offer much dialogue in return, but even a one-year-old or two-year-old child will benefit from having received your open display of love and hearing your words of truth. It's never too early to start building a bond of love and trust with your child.

And don't think that doing this one time is all that's necessary. Depending on your individual situation, you might need weekly talks, monthly talks, or annual times to visit with your child so that they know your love is consistent, strong, and unwavering. When they recognize that you are always eager to let them know how much they mean to you, they will begin to honor your role as their father, the leader of the household, and the foundational support of their life forever.

Once you are at your special location, simply open your heart and let your child know how you feel about being their father. Don't make small talk—just open right up and let your child know why it is you wanted to be there with them.

"I wanted to bring you here so we can have a special place for us to talk. I want you to know how important you are to my life as my child. Watching you grow and seeing the person you are becoming gives me a sense of pride and accomplishment as your father. I love you more than anything in this world, and I just want to make sure you know how I feel. I love being your father, and I love you with all my heart. I will always be here for you and want you to know you are never alone, no matter what you are going through in your life."

Put your arm around their shoulder or give them a close hug. Don't let go. Let your words soak in. Don't keep rambling on and on. Give them time to process what you've just said. Silence can be golden.

Depending on where you are in your relationship with your child, their response will vary. Don't expect them to say, "I love you too." They might. They might be so shocked at what you've just done that they won't know what to say. Try not to ask them too many questions about how they feel or what they think about what you said. Instead, focus on simply telling your child your true feelings. Be proud of your child and trust that God will give you the right words to say.

"I know it's a busy life and sometimes I get so overwhelmed with everything that I don't let you know how important you are to me, so I wanted to have some special time for us to get away from all of the distractions and let you know how happy I am to have you as my child. I'm sorry if I don't tell you enough or show you enough, but I love you unconditionally. I know you will be a great success someday, and I'm proud of all that you do."

You have now set the foundational cornerstone in your relationship with your child. Now that they know how you feel, they will have an instantaneous surge of love and respect for you because you have opened your heart and allowed them inside your emotional boundaries.

You might find this difficult to do the first time around. You might even find it a bit scary. But this is what your child needs from you. This is your responsibility as a father to let them know exactly what they mean to you and that you are there to love them through thick and thin. This will give your child a solid foundation to stand on for the rest of their life. They might seem bashful about accepting your words or embarrassed by your open display of affection, but deep inside, they will welcome your proclamation of love because it will give them a strong peace of mind and comfort in their heart. It will also help them open their heart up to you in return. And when both of you can share your feelings with one another, your relationship will bloom and become stronger than ever.

If you have more than one child, don't take them all out for a talk at the same time. Each child is their own person, and even though you love your children equally, you need to establish this open display of love with each of your children individually.

You will find that after you open your heart to your child, it will be easier to display your feelings in the future. Not only will this make your child feel better, but you will also feel better about the way you are able to speak with your child. The strength of your relationship will grow each time you tell them that you love them.

A father helps his child grow. Physically, emotionally, mentally, and spiritually.

A child is a seed that you have planted in the garden of Earth. Your words of love are the nutrients that will make them stand strong. Your actions of love are the rays of sunshine that will help them grow. Your loving support will help them remain straight and tall. God's love will help them bear good fruit to share with those around them.

If you do not supply words of love, they will not stand as strong. If you do not supply actions of love, they will not grow to their potential.

If you do not supply loving support, they will not remain straight and tall.

Without knowing God's love, they will not bear the fruit they were meant to yield.

When you openly demonstrate your love to your child, you are teaching them how to do the same. Setting a great example for your child to follow will help them learn how to treat others they meet throughout their life.

Step 4
EMBRACE YOUR CHILD

Men are not usually touchy-feely creatures who readily offer emotional support to others. Men shake hands, give pats on the back, high fives, and fist bumps—all of which are quick actions that require minimal contact with another person.

Of course, men will hold hands with their wives or offer them other small gestures of affection. For the most part, men are not naturally programmed to hug and hold loved ones. We are meant to protect our family, which means that we have always stood watch while our wives have held the children. It's okay for you to modify the traditional rules if it means having a stronger bond with your child.

When it comes to your child, you need to understand that the more you hug and hold them, the closer your relationship will become over time.

Every child grows at a different speed, both physically and emotionally, but they all go through the same developmental stages, and they all require the same type of nurturing. The more you touch and hold your child, the more support they will feel from you, and the stronger your bond will be.

A child's brain won't be able to make them say "Hold me, daddy," when they really need it. But they will welcome the warm feeling they receive from having your arms wrapped around them-- so do it often.

Even simple acts of putting your hand on their shoulder, rubbing their neck, or patting their thigh can serve to make them feel they are loved and cared for.

While it is important to strengthen these simple actions with words of love and encouragement, it's not always necessary to say something every time you give them a hug. Just make an effort to demonstrate to your child that you care about them.

If they want to show you something, like a school project or a report card, don't take it and look at it by yourself after they go to bed. Invite them to sit with you, put your arm around them, and be interested in what they are showing you. Embrace your child in multiple ways at the same time.

Eye contact and direct conversation, warm hugs and touches, welcoming comments, and supportive discussions can all be done at the same time. You must make a real effort to try and connect with your child on different levels so that they feel you are totally concentrating on them. You need to make them feel that at that moment in time, they are the single most important thing in your life.

If you are reading a book or scrolling through your phone when your child approaches, don't just put the book or phone down on your lap—put the item away. Bring your child onto your lap. Give your child your full attention.

If you are checking emails or texting on your personal device when your child approaches, don't say "Wait until I finish this," and then just keep on typing (unless you are doing something so important that it can't wait for three or four minutes). You must put your child at the top of your priority list. Put your device aside and say, "You're much more important than some work emails. Come here and sit with Daddy."

This does two things. First, it demonstrates to your child that they are your highest priority, and second, it communicates that you are glad to give them your undivided attention.

I'm sure you know that the human brain has two sides that control different human functions, both emotional and physical. You can make a child happy with your words, and that stimulates one side of their brain that processes what you say. You can also make a child happy with your hugs and kisses, and that stimulates the other side of their brain. If you can make them happy by talking to them and holding them at the same time, you are connecting with both sides of their brain simultaneously, and they will have a deeper connection to you.

Embracing your child involves both a mental and physical connection. You have to want to be interested in what your child is telling you, showing you, or asking you. Your child should not have to demand your full attention. Ignoring them will cause them to be more impatient. You should be the one to realize that your child is reaching out for you and make yourself readily available.

If you are working at home, try to conduct your business in a single room set aside for that purpose. You can tell your child that they need to understand that you sometimes have important work to do at home and that when you are in your "business area," they might have to wait a moment or so until you are free for them.

However, don't make your entire house your office or business area and don't stay in your business area all the time. This way, you can remain approachable for any reason in any part of your home and be able to give your immediate attention to your child's needs. Children want to be able to connect with you immediately, especially if you have been at work all day and away from home.

You are the security blanket for which they are longing. No matter how long and hard your workday was, don't put that burden on your child when you get home and walk through the door by saying, "Let daddy rest for a little while. It's been a long day." A child hears that differently. They hear, "You're not special enough for me to find the extra energy I need for you right now. My job is more important than you, and I don't really have much time for you right now."

The quickest way to damage your relationship with your child is to put them low on your list of priorities. You must be a father who puts your child first. All the time. Your child will soon feel like the most important person in your life and, strangely enough, won't be so needy all the time. When a child is constantly whining for your attention, it's their way of saying they need more of you. Be conscious of their needs and try your hardest to give them what they need from you as a father. Again, this doesn't mean giving them new sneakers every time they ask or giving them the latest phone or electronic gadget. It means giving them your love, attention, and affection at all times and telling them how you feel about them. Build them up in public, congratulate them in front of others, and give them words of encouragement when they are with their friends.

If you must instruct your child or correct their behavior, do it in private—not in front of their friends. Don't ridicule or embarrass them in front of their peers. Correct them with civil discussions rather than yelling or screaming. They are learning everything from you. They will treat others as you are treating them. Teaching your children to yell and scream will only make you yell and scream at them more for their loud behavior.

Make your child's happiness the top priority of your day. If you need some downtime after work, park your car around the block for ten or fifteen minutes and take a breather before walking through the front door. Unwind before you come home. As soon as you see your child, be prepared to greet them with open arms, a big smile, a warm hug, and loving and caring words. You will be the champion of their day.

The happiness that you give to your child by being enthusiastic to see them will become a highlight of their day. And yours as well.

Depending on the age of your child, you can develop a ritual greeting like a running hug and toss in the air, a hug and a tickle on the knee, or butterfly kisses—anything at all that makes the moment special when you walk through that door.

Older children might think this is corny or silly, but they will eventually understand that this is a way for you to communicate to them that "I am here for you, and I am interested in what you did today." Unlike the time when you hold your special talk, this is a perfectly good time to ask them questions about their friends and about their day. Listen to their answers. Don't get sidetracked with phone calls, texting, or other things. Devote your attention to your child. Phones have voicemail for a reason. Human interaction is vital and can't simply be recaptured or replayed in the moment. Make your child your top priority, and you will be greatly rewarded.

When my daughter was very young and when I was putting her down for bedtime, I would tell her "Eenie Meanie Chili Beanie, Daddy wishes you sweet dreamy." Thirty years later, we still send messages of "Eenie Meanie" at bedtime. Create a special ritual with your child and it will last a lifetime.

At the same time, you will be building an emotional connection with your child that will get stronger each day. This daily ritual will make an indelible mark on your child's subconscious mind and give them positive memories of you and your relationship together for the rest of their life.

When you show them you care, you also transform yourself so that you really do care, which will help make you a loving Christian father.

Step 5
SUPPORT YOUR CHILD

As a loving Christian father, you must be able to instill confidence in your child. The support structure you provide for them will be an important part of their personal development and success as they progress through life.

They'll need your support in many different areas of their life including parental support, financial support, moral support, emotional support, mental support, and religious and spiritual support. Not only will they need your support, but you will also have to give that support to your children unconditionally and without hesitation. That doesn't mean that you must automatically say yes to their every need and desire, but when the time comes that they need to depend on you, you must be ready to quickly step forward and provide the appropriate comfort.

When your child is just learning to walk, you will support them as they take those first few wobbly steps. Just feeling the support of your hands will give your child the carefree confidence they need to take steps on their own. They will reach up for your hands even before they can talk because they understand that you are there to assist and support them.

They need your strength at all ages during their growth and development.

When your child learns to ride a bike or a skateboard, they will depend on you to support them and provide the proper guidance that allows them to find the right balance. They will beg you to not let go as they make the first few pedals, and then suddenly they will be screaming for you to let go so they can do it on their own.

That is the constant struggle you will face as a loving Christian father for your entire life. How long should you hold on and when should you let go?

When you take your child to their first day of school, your support will reassure them that you will be there when they finish the day. There might be tears of separation and a little anxiety (theirs and yours both), but that feeling will soon fade away and be replaced by confidence to face the school day alone.

Obviously, depending on your job, you can't be there each and every day to take them to school and pick them up, but you should do whatever it takes to make sure that you and your wife are there every day for the first week of kindergarten and the first week of each grade school year after that. This will give them a sense of confidence and security. After the first week, you can alternate with your wife or other family members, but it is vitally important that you, the father, be there at least sometimes to drop them off and pick them up at school to reinforce a strong and consistent support structure.

When your child learns to jump from a diving board, your outstretched arms will provide the support that allows them to make the leap of faith into the water. Don't force your child to jump or dive and don't embarrass them or ridicule them. They depend on you for support, and they need your positive encouragement. They will make the leap when they are ready, and then they will no longer need you there. But if you force the issue, they will do it before they are ready and forever have a negative memory of that first jump into freedom, which will make them forever cautious about taking such a risk in the future.

Forcing your child to do something they aren't comfortable with can cause developmental issues for many years to come. Every child is different and progresses at a different pace. Just because their friends are doing things at a certain age doesn't mean that your child is comfortable with doing the same thing yet. Be supportive and they will blossom when they are ready. Every child is a unique individual, and there is no predetermined timetable for what they should be doing at a particular age. God created them as individuals with their own habits and eccentricities just like He created you.

These may seem like small milestones in life but consider what would happen if you weren't there to offer your support. There are many things that can go wrong in the early developmental stages of a child's life that can adversely impact their confidence and mental growth.

A loving Christian father is one who has time, patience, and an understanding of what a child feels when they are faced with a new and sometimes fearful situation.

As adults, we have had time to experience challenges in life that might seem to be no big deal. A three-foot diving board might seem like a piece of cake to you and me since we are grown adults, but to a small child, those three feet of space staring at them in the face might as well be a ten-story building because they haven't had a chance to adjust. Understand where your child's mind is and offer the proper support.

Your positive support will help them overcome their doubts and fears. Don't make the situation worse by yelling or belittling them. And never compare them to other children. "What are you afraid of? Bobby did it." What a child hears is "Bobby is a better child because he was able to do something you won't do."

Supporting your child doesn't mean letting them do anything they want. You wouldn't support a child's decision to throw rocks at a window. You wouldn't support a child's decision to play with guns. You must make sure your child knows that you are always there for them no matter what—as long as they are making the right moral and ethical choices you expect them to make on a daily basis. And that they respect the rules of your house.

You must also let them know that your support is based on an honest and truthful relationship between the two of you. Explain that there might come a day when they are accused of dishonesty, maybe even at school. If your child is truthful, no matter whether they're guilty or not, let them know you will be there to support them and see that the problem is resolved. If your child is not honest, let them know your support will be overshadowed by their dishonesty and that disciplinary measures will need to be enforced.

Every child goes through a phase of dishonesty. The falsehood usually results from your child not wanting to get in trouble and not wanting to provoke your anger. Most children grow out of this phase quickly when they learn that there are strict consequences for not being truthful.

By giving the proper support to your child from an early age, you will instill confidence in them so that they can make the correct moral and ethical choices in life. When they know that they can count on you, it will give them a tremendous boost to face the difficult choices they will encounter as they grow up.

On the other hand, if you are always leaving them in doubt about how you feel about them when they disappoint you, they will lack the self-confidence necessary to make tough decisions. Your child needs to know that you will always be there to support them in whatever they choose to do. We all make mistakes, but you have to allow your child the leeway to make decisions instead of always telling them what to do and how to act.

Observe your child and see how they react to different circumstances. Give them the chance to figure things out on their own. Give them the freedom to make the right choice, and when they do, compliment them for doing the right thing. If you are always telling them everything to do and how to behave, they will not develop the ability to think things through because they will always be waiting for you to correct them or advise them. When they hear you always telling them what they did was wrong, all they ever hear are negative things about them, which will surely cause them internal pain and hurt feelings. Fill their life with positive, supportive comments that make them feel good about themselves.

You have been there since their inception and their birth, and your presence gives them confidence and comfort at the same time to make the right choices in life. Even when you are not physically there, your child will draw on your support and will know in their heart how you would want them to react. They will make the right choices because they know you will be pleased by their behavior.

Even though most children are not physically delivered into the world until after ten months of pregnancy, your baby is already able to sense the outside world from deep inside your wife's womb. Your baby can hear your voice, your baby can feel movement, and your baby can feel your love.

Have you ever been in an apartment and heard a loud argument coming from the neighbors next door? The thin wall that separates the apartments allows you to hear the shouts and the yells and the screams and the crashing furniture, and your imagination runs wild as you consider what must be going on over there. The scene is completely out of your control, but you feel the violence and the anxiety from the argument as it invades your inner peace.

Babies experience the exact same thing every moment of their development in the womb. If you are mad at your wife and the two of you are arguing and fighting and your wife is in tears because you are not getting along, your baby is being subjected to the fight too. People think that because the baby hasn't been born yet, that the baby can't sense what's going on. But your baby, even while still inside the womb, has already developed the ability to hear, and they are experiencing every emotional moment between you and your wife.

A baby inside the womb needs to have a calm, quiet, loving environment so that they can develop a warm, calm personality. Loud crashing noises, arguments, shouts, screams, slamming doors, and other violent outbursts will surely create a nervous environment for your baby that will cause them to be a nervous infant once they are born.

Think about your own peace of mind. How would you like it if you were asleep, snuggled in a warm blanket, when suddenly you were rudely awakened by slamming doors and loud arguments and then getting bounced around in your bed from one direction to the next?

That's precisely the same feeling your baby will have if your wife is pacing a room in an intense argument with you.

During both of my wife's pregnancies, I used to lay my head next to her belly and get as close as I could to my unborn baby. I would talk to my baby in a deep, soothing voice every night before we went to bed. I would read books aloud and gently rub my wife's belly. I made this a ritual so that my child would recognize my voice from its earliest stages of inception all the way through its birth.

I was in the delivery room for the birth of both of my children. When my first child was born and I heard him cry aloud, I stepped close to the nurse and spoke to my child in the same soothing voice I had been using for the past few months. My son stopped crying and turned his head in my direction as he recognized my voice. I'm convinced that the familiar sound he had heard every night let him know that his father was there to comfort him and to welcome him into the world.

Keeping your emotions in check and keeping your wife happy during your pregnancy is extremely important to raising a well-balanced child. When your wife understands that you are with her, heart and soul, throughout the pregnancy, the bond you will build together will help provide a stable environment for your baby to thrive in.

And the joy that you will share with your wife during this difficult time will make the experience that much more loving and rewarding for you both as you share God's gift of life that has been given to you.

When you are in the delivery room with your wife, you will be blessed with the most emotional high of your life as your baby is brought into the world right in front of you. And as you see your newborn child for the first time, you will know that you have the greatest responsibility a man can ever have—to give that baby love and care for the rest of its life.

By the grace of God, you will be sent a babe to hold in your arms, a child who will need you and love you unconditionally every minute of every day, so long as you provide the love, care, protection, sustenance, and guidance that a loving Christian father needs to give them so that they feel loved and wanted.

You are the man who must give them the love that they need so that they will not feel alone in the world. You are the man who must give them the safety of your protective arms to wrap around them so that they'll never fear anything if you are with them. You must be the man who is there each morning as they awaken and are there each night when they go to sleep, providing them the security of a stable family structure that tells them you are always there for them no matter what.

Your child also needs to know that you realize they are not perfect, you don't expect them to be perfect, and that everyone makes mistakes. God forgives those who ask for forgiveness, just as a loving Christian father forgives their wayward child when they seek forgiveness.

Step 6
LEAD YOUR CHILD BY YOUR CHRISTIAN BEHAVIOR

Imitation is the sincerest form of flattery. Monkey see, monkey do. Watch and learn.

Throughout time, experience shows us that we learn better by watching others. Children learn from other children, and they also learn from adults, especially from their parents.

As a loving Christian father, you have to realize that your child will be watching everything you do. When an infant is old enough to open their eyes, they start recognizing visual images. That is one of the ways that a baby can differentiate Mommy and Daddy from other adults. A young baby begins to recognize familiar people and objects in the early stages of life and keeps those visual images in their brain for later use.

You can imagine how important it is for you to act as you want your child to act. Your behavior will be watched by your child for years, so you have to be careful about what sort of visual signals you send to your child during their formative years.

If you haven't considered this in advance, your child may have already stored negative behavioral patterns in their brain. The trouble is that these patterns do not materialize until much later when they are more difficult to correct.

For instance, if you are a smoker, your subliminal message to your child is that it is a natural thing to have a cigarette in your hand and blow smoke from your lips. You might be the kind of smoker who at least smokes outside to prevent your child's exposure to second-hand smoke. Maybe you even step outside the sliding glass doors so you can keep an eye on the child while you "sneak a smoke."

If you can see your child, they can see you. And when your child watches you day after day, week after week, and year after year smoking a cigarette, the child will grow up with a mental picture that smoking is normal. They might be too young to understand an explanation of the dangers of smoking and that you don't want them to smoke, but you have already preconditioned your child with your actions and the mental images that you approve of smoking.

The same goes for drinking alcohol, overeating, physical abuse, rude language, anger, and a whole list of other negative behaviors. Your child has a video recorder for a brain, and that brain has a fresh hard drive in it that will record everything they see you do. They might be too young to recall early memories, but those images and experiences go a long way to influence future behavior.

Therefore, in order for you to have the best chance of successfully raising a respectful, loving child, you must portray the image of a respectful, loving father.

"Do you not know that you are God's temple and that God's Spirit dwells in you? If anyone destroys God's temple, God will destroy him. For God's temple is holy, and you are that temple" (1 Corinthians 3:16-17 ESV).

If you have a habit of using profanity, your children will find it easy to use the same language because you have taught them through repetition. You don't have to sit them at a desk and give them lessons on how to use four-letter words; profanity will naturally become a part of their vernacular if it's a regular part of yours. They want to sound like Daddy.

When children are comfortable with using profanity, they are less respectful to those around them, and they will develop attitude problems that will follow them through their school years. If you are using profanity around your children, even occasionally, then your children will use the same words in similar situations in their own lives. Then one day, during an important meeting or interview, your child will let those familiar words slip and no doubt, will spoil any chances of making a positive impression due to their casual use of profanity. It is important to realize that parenting results in a clone of yourself that will become part of the next generation, and you have to be incredibly careful about what traits you are giving to your child.

I believe that all children want to be just like their parents in so many ways. The child sees the parent as having the ultimate authority in the house, so they assume that whatever the parent is doing must be good. The child does not realize that negative behavior is bad for them when they see the adults in their life doing the same thing.

When my son was about a year and a half old, I was painting the walls in our house, and it was just the two of us in the living room. My son was playing with some toys nearby and watching as I used a paint roller to paint up and down the walls. As I was working, the telephone rang, so I set the roller on the pan and answered the phone for a short conversation.

A few moments later, I noticed that it had gotten quiet in the room, and when I turned around, my son was standing in the middle of the room, holding the paint roller in his hand just like he had seen his daddy doing. Before I could react, he bent down and rolled out three big, white paint stripes—right on the gray carpet.

I remember thinking at the time, *If I yell at him to stop, I'll scare him and probably scar him for a long time.* So, I calmly walked over and said, "Boy, you did a great job of painting. Come over here and do it on this wall." And I let him paint with the roller on the wall. It didn't matter if he was doing it the right way; it mattered that I let him do the same thing he had just seen me doing.

I think about this from time to time, and I realize I was breaking the mold of how my father would have handled that same situation. I'm sure I would have gotten a spanking or gotten yelled at by my dad, so I pat myself on the back for having a positive reaction to a negative event. Besides, it wasn't his fault that I left the paint roller on the floor within his reach, so why should he have gotten in trouble? He saw Daddy doing something that looked like fun, and he wanted to do the same thing. I didn't have to tell him how to use the roller. He just watched and learned all on his own at the ripe old age of eighteen months.

You never know when your child will be watching you and what will make an impression on them. It's best to assume that they are always watching and that you are teaching your child through everything you do.

I've seen many video clips of young children doing inappropriate things that the parents think is cute, such as saying a bad word or making a rude gesture. Some parents are actually proud of their child's bad behavior, posting it all over social media, and those parents should not be surprised when their child gets in trouble at school for using bad words and making rude gestures towards other students and teachers. Those children have been conditioned to understand that their bad behavior gets giggles and laughs from their parents at an early age, so it's only natural for them to continue thinking that the best way to get laughs and giggles is to continue doing the same thing.

Bad habits are extremely hard to break.

If you want your child to use good manners, then you have to demonstrate good manners in your daily interactions.

If you want your child to say prayers before meals and at bedtime, then you need to pray in front of them and show them the right way to talk to God.

A loving Christian father will set the right example for their child in language, manner, attitude, beliefs, and every other aspect of your child's life that you find important.

Don't let your negative behavior or habits be an influence on your child. You must show your child the right way to live, and over time, the positive images you project will reinforce acceptable behaviors and habits.

Even if you weren't raised by positive adult role models, you are the adult now in your child's life. You must have the maturity to give them the best help and advice possible to make them a success in life. Lead by example so your child will follow the right path.

Step 7
COMMUNICATE WITH YOUR CHILD

A loving Christian father must be able to communicate well with his children. Communication is a two-way dialogue. It is just as important to listen as it is to speak.

Have you ever met someone for the first time, and then a few minutes later, you can't remember their name? The reason is simple. Most people are usually more interested in telling someone their own name rather than learning the other person's name.

To solve this problem, when you meet someone and hear their name for the first time, use their name right away three different ways. Such as "Hi Tom. Hey Tom, where are you from? What kind of work do you do, Tom?" When you repeat their name three times, you won't forget it because you are trying to make the effort to remember their name.

Communicating with your child effectively requires the same active listening skills. When you speak to your child and they are trying to ask you something important, or when they want to do something you're not so wild about, repeat their phrase back to them in a few different ways BEFORE deciding how to answer them.

This serves multiple purposes: First, it allows you to clearly understand what they are asking and demonstrates that you are tuned in to their conversation. Secondly, it gives you a moment to run the options through your brain before answering right away. Sometimes we are so preprogrammed to say no that we answer without really thinking things through.

Oftentimes, after saying no immediately, the parent finally gives in after further discussion and changes their mind. This trains the child that no does not really mean *no*—it is merely a bargaining point to be argued until a more favorable decision can be negotiated in the child's favor.

When you say no, you should mean *no*, so only say no after you're certain you actually mean *no*.

Nobody likes to get shot down immediately. When a child asks for something and your immediate response is "No," or "I'll think about it," that is telling your child you don't really want to take the question seriously, which will frustrate them. However, repeating the question a couple of times back to them shows that you are trying to understand and that you are considering the options, which will make your child feel like you care.

You can still say no. But at least you will have taken a moment to weigh the options. Also, when you tell your child no, it's best to try and clarify the reason why whenever possible.

"Can Betty spend the night?" your child asks.

You reply, "You want Betty to spend the night? Hmmm. Can Betty spend the night? Do you realize it's a school night? And you haven't even started your homework because you've been playing video games since you got home. Maybe it's better to do it on another night when you have your homework completed earlier."

Your child might not like the answer, but at least they can understand your reasoning. If you just say no right away, your child might not grasp the full reasoning behind your answer.

I'm sure you've heard a parent say, "I said no, and that's the only reason you need, because I said so." That's an abrupt answer that almost always causes a negative reaction because there's no real reasoning behind the answer except "I'm bigger, and I'm the adult, and you have to do it my way." Children are inquisitive and always looking at how things work, and an absolute answer like that does nothing to answer their question in a rational way that they can understand. So, they will ask the same question repeatedly until you blow a circuit or eventually give in.

If you answer your child's question with some additional information, you will be helping them learn how to evaluate situations by understanding the information required to make the correct decision. Do you want a child that merely follows instructions, or do you want a child that understands why they are getting the instructions and then agrees to follow them? The first one is a soldier; the second one is a general.

This is a better way to communicate. Don't make your child read your mind and guess what you are thinking. Be clear with your reasoning, and you will have fewer confrontations about the decisions you make for your child. This will also teach your child to add details to their communications with you. The more information and reasoning your child provides, the easier it is for you to process their request. Let your child know this so they can help themselves in the future.

When communicating with your child, give them your undivided attention. I spoke about this earlier in Step 4. It is so important to put aside whatever you are doing and zero in on your child's conversation, so they feel you care about them.

Similarly, do not allow your child to try and communicate with you about important issues when they are distracted either. If they are texting or on the computer while asking you about something important, ask them for their undivided attention so you can have a clear line of communication with each other. It's okay to explain to them that you want to make sure you are both on the same page, and it is easier if you both are paying attention to each other.

Don't start a conversation and then ask them to put their phone away. Ask them to put the phone away *first* and then have your conversation. This gives them a chance to complete what they are doing, and it won't seem like you are cutting in unfairly and pushing your agenda on them.

Good communication skills are soon going to be harder to find in this world, especially with the popularity of texting and instant messaging. Kids are more apt to send a text than they are to make a call. Don't fall into the trap of letting your child text you about every situation. Make them call and have verbal conversations with you. If they text you, call them back to speak to them. You can ask many more questions over the phone in the amount of time it takes to read a text and respond.

During a phone call, you can also hear what is happening in the background. If your child is at a loud party and sends a text that they are at a friend's house, you might not get the real picture from simply reading a text. With a phone call, you might be able to hear the loud party and quickly recognize they are not at a friend's house doing homework. Today, every bit of information you can gather when your child is out and about will serve you better in the long run.

An open line of communication with your child will make your relationship stronger and allow you to build trust with each other.

Step 8
DISCIPLINE YOUR CHILD

Do the crime, do the time.

It might be hard to imagine but think about what kind of world we would live in if there were no rules and no punishment. Wow. People would get away with all kinds of things and never worry about having to pay any sort of penalty.

As a loving Christian father, one of the hardest things you will have to do is discipline your child. Nobody likes to put someone through the pain of disciplinary measures, especially since we have all endured discipline ourselves to varying degrees.

The sooner you begin to discipline your child, the less you will have to do it.

Say that again?

I am a firm believer that if you can establish structured discipline early on in your child's life, you will have fewer problems with them as they grow older. You will also have to use fewer punishments.

Set your discipline structure and remain steadfast in enforcing it on a consistent basis. Don't resort to one strategy for a while, switch to a new strategy, and then change back to the original strategy again. Your child must know your boundary lines, and those boundary lines must remain consistent throughout their life. Otherwise, if they know the rules change from time to time, they will push to change the rules anytime they disagree with your boundaries.

In a football game, the sidelines are the sidelines. If you go out of bounds, the clock stops, and the play is over. If players could move the sidelines anytime they wanted to, chaos would happen. The runner would always be running out of bounds to avoid getting hit, and they would just keep on running. More importantly, they would be getting hit more because the defenders would have to try and stop them out of bounds since the sidelines were meaningless.

The same thing holds true for your child. If you allow them to run out of your boundaries without a penalty, they will always run out of bounds. This will cause them to run farther and farther out of bounds, which will make you penalize them even harder than normal because you will be shocked at how far they will go.

Set your boundary lines and let your child know what they are. You need to communicate clearly so that there is no misunderstanding about what the rules are. Don't make them read your mind or guess what you mean. If you do not establish the boundaries precisely as you mean them, your child will push and push to bend and break the rules.

That's the way the discipline game is played between parents and children. Stick to your rules and your life will be easier than if you keep changing the rules to make your children happy. A few things are certain to happen:

I promise you that your child will try to bend and break your rules.

I promise you that you will have to discipline your child.

It will be up to you how many times your child breaks your rules, and that depends on how consistent you are with discipline and punishment and at what age you get serious about defending your rules. No matter what, your rules should also be age-appropriate for your child.

Allowing a young child to stay up until midnight on a school night is not age-appropriate.

Conversely, making an older child go to bed at seven o'clock on a Friday night is also not age-appropriate (unless it is for disciplinary reasons).

You must understand that discipline needs to be instilled in your children at an early age.

When my son was just a little over one-year-old, he was laying on his back as I was changing his diaper and he started kicking at me. I put my hands on his feet and told him to stop. He was staring right into my eyes as I was talking to him, and I know he understood me completely because as soon as I leaned a little more forward, he got a sly grin on his face and kicked me hard right in the chest.

I raised his leg in the air and gave him one little swat on the behind and told him no.

Did I just really say that?

Yes, I spanked a one-year-old with one light swat on the behind.

You might think he was too young to understand. I'd say you just had to be there to see how he stared me in the eye and how deliberate he was in cocking his leg back and delivering the kick. I gave him the boundary—no kicking. He ran out of bounds and kicked me. Penalty time—one small swat.

He didn't kick me again.

I immediately felt terrible right after that happened. I had reacted to his kick and had swatted him before I knew what I had done. Fortunately, it was only one small swat. But I had done it without really thinking about it. And you know why?

Because that's the way my parents disciplined me. And suddenly I found myself near tears as I recalled the punishments I received from my parents in my early days. My parents both came from the old-school method of spanking with belts, switches, and openhanded slaps. Occasionally, they would grab anything close, like a telephone or a stick, and whack you with it. Sometimes my dad even balled up his fists and dared me to hit him back when I rebelled at his punishments.

I remember how frightened I was of my dad, never knowing how he would react to something I did wrong and what item he would use as his "enforcer." I remember with dread riding in the car and him saying, "Just wait till we get home—you're going to get it good." Still makes my stomach do backflips to this day just thinking about it.

I swore I would never make my child feel that same sick feeling of fear in his stomach like I did. Or have my child grown up being deathly afraid of me like I was of my dad.

I was not going to be like my father. I wanted to break the mold.

That's when I decided to sit down and think about discipline and punishment for my children. It's not something you really prepare yourself for. But, believe me, you should. Just like you set your boundary lines for your child, you should set your own boundary lines for yourself and what type of punishment structure you are going to use in your family. Trust me, you will need it.

Let me visit with you for a moment about swats, spankings, time-outs, and groundings. There are all sorts of books written by people with all kinds of degrees that will support any position you want to take when it comes to what method of punishment works best on kids.

What I can tell you is that every child is different, and you are going to have to set your own policy in your own household to find what works best. When I was growing up, I was a free spirit with a vivid imagination (I left home without permission and had a hard time telling the truth).

Not to say I didn't deserve a little straightening out every now and then, but you have to admit that belts, sticks, and branches are rather extreme items to punish a child with. I even remember one time that I got tied to a tree for a couple of hours in the front yard because I went across the street without asking permission.

In today's world, using these items to discipline a child would get a person arrested and charged with child abuse. But, back in my childhood, it was a different world.

I was in my mid-thirties when I had my first baby, so I had a lot of time to reflect on discipline and punishment and how it had affected me as I was growing up. I'm sure my dad beat me because his dad beat him because his dad beat him, and it had been passed down through the generations of my forefathers back to the early days of "spare the rod and spoil the child."

I made an oath to myself that I would never do things like that to my children, no matter what they did.

I decided I was going to break the mold. I made a promise to myself that if I ever had to spank my child, I would only use my bare hand and swat them only on their rear. One swat when they were one-year-old.

Two swats when they were two. Three swats when they were three. And that's the most I would ever swat them with my bare hand. Three swats.

I also made a promise to myself that I would not lash out in anger, but that if a swat were necessary, I would explain to them why they were going to get punished BEFORE they were punished so they would understand the reason. This way they would be able to clearly see the boundary line and where they had stepped outside of it. They would know the penalty before it was enforced so they wouldn't make the same mistake again.

And most important of all, after they got their punishment, I promised myself to hug them and hold them close and tell them I loved them and that I was not mad at them.

I've heard some experts say that by hitting a child, you teach a child to hit. I want to make it clear that I never hit my children.

I never beat my children. I never swatted them with my full strength.

But my young children did receive structured discipline as they were growing up. I can probably think of three or four times my son got swats before he was in the seventh grade. My daughter got swats maybe two or three times. And neither of my children grew up to be hitters, bullies, or violent children.

My children also got time-outs. They were sent to their bedrooms.

They were grounded. They had their phones taken away.

What I'm trying to say here is that you have to be flexible in the methods you choose so that the punishment fits the situation and their age. Not every offense has to be a "swat-able" offense, and you certainly don't want that to be your reaction 100 percent of the time.

My wife and I disagreed about the structured discipline for our children since she did not believe in spankings. Her philosophy was lectures and time-outs. We had our disagreements about this as the children were growing up, but I held firm to my belief that sometimes swats were necessary, and so I was the disciplinarian of our family.

They were not afraid of me as a father. They were afraid of the punishment. That's why the boundaries and punishment are there. As a deterrent to recurring bad decisions.

I wanted my children to know that if they crossed the boundary line, they would get penalized. It didn't take them long to learn that if they stayed in bounds, they could play and have as much fun as they wanted, and things were great for us all.

Set your rules and make them clear. Write them down, if necessary, especially with older children. Leave no wiggle room for misunderstanding. If there's a loophole in your rules, your child will find it and exploit it.

Enforce the rules fairly for all children. Do not let one child get away with something that another child has previously been punished for. Don't punish one child more harshly for doing the same thing another child has done previously.

Set your discipline structure and make sure both parents consistently enforce it as much as possible. Otherwise, children will soon learn to play parents against each other. You must have a unified front.

If there are times when you and your wife do not agree on structured discipline, take a few minutes to discuss your different points of view. If after further consideration you still believe you are right, you should proceed ahead and carry out your plan. Raise your children the best way you see fit. You are the father.

You have the right to be one.

Never punish your child in a way that is abusive, demeaning, humiliating, or dangerous. You can have permanent negative effects on your child by using any of these methods.

Never discipline your child in front of friends or relatives. Remove yourself and your child from the immediate scene and go to a closed room where you and the child can communicate clearly with one another.

Do not "double discipline" your child. If one parent has already given the child a punishment, let that serve as the punishment. You can discuss the situation with your child so that they understand your position, but after the discussion, end the meeting with a hug and positive words of encouragement.

Do not allow any other caretaker, babysitter, sibling, or relative to discipline your child other than you and your wife. Your child should only answer to you and your wife so that you can control and modify your child's behavior in a consistent manner.

A tree that starts growing crooked at an early age needs to be straightened as soon as possible. The longer the tree grows crooked, the more difficult it is to straighten until finally it cannot be straightened at all.

"Poverty and disgrace come to those who ignore discipline, but the one who accepts correction will be honored" (Proverbs 13:18 CSB).

Step 9
BE POSITIVE WITH YOUR CHILD

A college class held a psychology experiment. Everyone in the class was in on the experiment except for one student. Throughout the class and throughout the morning, several students approached the one "study subject" and made comments like "Are you feeling okay?" "Gee, you look a little pale. Are you okay?" "Are you coming down with something?"

Before too long, the study subject was in the bathroom feeling queasy and ready to get sick to their stomach—all because of the outside suggestions of the other students. There was nothing wrong with the study subject at all, but the verbal insinuations that something wasn't right actually had a negative reaction on the student's well-being.

In the same way, you will have a dramatic impact on your child's development simply by the way you speak and act around them. Just think about how many hours of involvement you'll clock in your child's life as they grow up. Your words and actions toward your child can send them on the road to success and fill them with confidence or cause them to lead a sheltered life of insecurity and underachievement.

Even hearing only one or two negative statements a month can cause a child to take them to heart, affecting them in ways you might never imagine.

And you might not even think the things you are saying are bad or negative. Your child might not ever tell you that they don't like the statements. In fact, they might not even consciously know it bothers them. But, over time, the damage to your child's development can be huge. You must think about what you say and how you say it. This is especially true with jokes about a child's looks, mannerisms, or habits.

A rule of thumb I have always followed is that once is funny, twice is irritating, and three times is bullying. One of the hardest things to learn as a parent is when NOT to say something funny.

Words can cut deeply and take forever to heal.

"Fathers, do not embitter your children, or they will become discouraged" (Colossians 3:21 NIV).

Have you ever been to an underground cavern and seen stalactites or stalagmites? These huge lime formations are caused by water—ONE DROP AT A TIME. Granted, the formation process takes countless years, but the continual action of one drop after another builds up and eventually causes a huge formation.

The same thing happens internally to a child who hears negative comments or gets teased all the time. "He's not a very good reader." "She has problems with math." "Why can't you run fast like your brother?"

A loving Christian father needs to focus on a child's positive attributes and always offer positive reinforcement. It's okay to tell your child "You're the best runner I've ever seen," even if he's not. It's okay for you to praise your child and praise them often. You are that child's energy source.

Your child wants to be the highlight of your life and will do everything they can to please you so they can hear those positive comments from you. Just like a puppy that chases the ball and brings it back for a simple pat on the head and occasional treat, your child lives for the moment when they know they please you.

God has given you a wonderful gift of a child, and He has given you the unfettered ability to raise that child as you see fit. You should want to honor God with your ability to praise your child at all times and to help them develop physically and emotionally into a strong, confident adolescent.

Your goal in child-rearing should be preparing them as well as humanly possible for the life in front of them. Your positive attitude and comments will make your child thrive and succeed in a world that feeds on negativity and failure.

Watch the news or read social media. How many positive stories are there about good things? Not many. There is enough hostility and disapproval in the world without your child having to hear it coming from you.

Build your child up at every opportunity you have. Each day you should be telling your child how proud you are of them and why. You should tell them how much you love them and why. You should tell them how good they are at something and how that will help them be a success in the future. You should tell them you love the way they behave. That you love watching them grow up into a young man or young lady.

Your actions and words establish the foundation that your child will base their personality and self-respect on. When you make your children feel good about themselves, they will carry themselves well, behave properly, and perform appropriately because you have given them your verbal approval that they are behaving like you want them to.

Don't be bashful with positive words or affection for your child. Just as a plant needs sunlight and nourishment, you are the main source of mental nourishment for your child. Every word of praise is a ray of sunshine that will allow them to grow.

You should love being a father. It has so many beautiful moments. Make sure your priorities are in the right order. At this point in your life, your own personal success should be low on your list of priorities, and the emotional growth and success of your child should be at the very top. Be a Christian leader in your community. Be a positive father to your children. Be a great husband to your wife. If you try your hardest to accomplish these three things, you will be rewarded many times over throughout all the days of your life.

You only have one chance to raise this child, so seize the moment, welcome the challenge, and perform to the best of your ability so that one day you can look back and tell yourself that you did everything possible to make a positive Christian environment for them.

Don't complain about things in front of your children. Don't argue with your wife in front of your children. Don't talk badly about your wife, friends, or relatives in front of your children. Don't discuss family financial difficulties in front of your children (unless you are teaching them economics or how to use a bank account). Keep your problems away from your children so they are not burdened by your worries. Adults have a different capacity for stress than children do, so protect them from unnecessary situations that might have a negative impact on them.

Your children are fragile. Always remember that. Until they are old enough to be in the world on their own, save them from the worldly problems and worries for as long as possible. Do always be honest with your children, but make any honest revelations age-appropriate. Just because they ask a tough question doesn't mean you have to give them every detail.

One time I was driving the car, and my son was about six years old and strapped into his car seat behind me. Unexpectedly he said, "Daddy, how do I get the baby seeds out of my penis?" First, I was proud of myself that I didn't crash the car. Secondly, I wondered who had taught him the word penis because I knew it wasn't me. I asked him how he knew about baby seeds in his penis, and he told me that Mommy had told him about the baby seeds and that Mommy had also told him that he should ask me how babies were made. Gee—thanks mom.

If he had been a few years older, I might have had a more straightforward answer about sex education, but at six years old, he still had his innocence to protect. But to maintain our bond of honesty, I still had to tell him the truth as best as I could. A truth that his six-year-old mind could understand.

So I told him that the baby seeds were inside of his body and that they came out of his penis much like when he went pee-pee, except that there was a switch inside of his body that decided whether baby seeds or pee-pee would come out and that when he was old enough, God would give him the ability to flip the switch to make baby seeds.

He was perfectly satisfied with that answer, and I had given him the truth, yet I spared him the intimate details about sexual intercourse that weren't necessary or appropriate at that age.

So, give your children honest answers and give them your positive support. They will always love and respect you for it.

"But anyone who lives by the truth comes to the light, so that his works may be shown to be accomplished by God" (John 3:21 CSB).

Step 10
GUIDE YOUR CHILD TO CHRIST

Have you ever held a horse on the end of a rope? If you face the horse and try to pull it forward, the horse will refuse and fight to move backward. However, if you turn your back to the horse and simply walk forward while holding the rope with a steady hand, the horse will gladly fall in step and be led without difficulty.

While a child is not the same thing as a horse, leading your child to Christ is actually a lot like leading a horse. Gentle, persuasive actions get better results than confrontational tugging and pulling.

A child's attention span and ability to process information changes dramatically from year to year as they get older. In the early years of a child's life, they do not have the reasoning ability to understand the full impact of giving their life to Christ.

Don't be in a rush to have your child baptized to make yourself feel like a loving Christian father. While it is important to counsel your child and provide the correct information on matters of faith and the Bible, it should be your child's decision to follow Christ.

That doesn't mean that you can't prompt your child to action but be careful not to insist on any sort of deadline for them to reach a decision. The best thing you can do is to surround your child with the type of lifestyle that promotes Christian values. If the environment is loving and caring and reflects your Christian beliefs, your child will come to realize how important the decision to become a Christian is and will make the choice to be saved.

As my children were growing up, I made sure to let them know that my wife and I loved them always. Also, that God loved them and gave them to us as a blessing. I had many conversations with them in which I explained the strength of a Christian family and how we had the promise of eternal life through the message of faith from Jesus Christ our Lord and Savior.

Many of these conversations took place at bedtime as the kids were snuggled under the covers ready to drift off to sleep. I chose that time to share with them because it helped reassure them of the peace and safety they had in their lives, not only from their mother and I, but also from God. When a child feels safe and secure, they sleep better and are fully rested when they wake up the next morning, ready to face a new day. Sharing a prayer at bedtime with your child gives them peace of mind that you are petitioning God for their safety and well-being. When they know that their earthly father is working alongside their heavenly Father to protect them from harm and injury, they'll develop an internal tranquility that will help build their Christian character.

As you demonstrate your own relationship with God and Jesus, your children will begin to develop their own relationship and come to understand how important it is to walk with God in their life. They will begin to ask more questions, which creates more opportunities for you to teach them how to communicate with God, so they are spiritually strong and prepared to nurture their own relationship with God. Do your part as a Christian father to offer words of advice and support so that your child is led down the right path to salvation. Your gentle words of how to form a relationship with God will set a strong foundation in your child so that they will want to include God in their life.

Don't scare your child at bedtime with stories of sin and burning in hell if they don't follow Christ, as this will undoubtedly cause worries and restless nights for your child. Don't give them too much information. Simply reinforce the fact that God loves them without any conditions attached and that you love them the same way. Concentrate on teaching your children the positive aspects of a relationship with God and let them make the decision to accept Jesus Christ as their Lord and Savior on their own. Don't push them to reach an answer or pester them about when they will be ready to be baptized. If you continue to provide a good example by your words and actions, they will make the decision for themselves at a time when they believe it is right.

I was raised as an independent Christian and went to church on a regular basis. My mom had wanted to join a church closer to our home when I was around ten years old, so when she walked forward to join the church with my older sister and I, I remember the preacher asking me a couple of questions, and the next thing I knew, I was being dunked underwater right along with my sister.

I knew I had been baptized, but it never really felt right because it didn't seem like my own decision. For years I had mixed emotions about whether I was fully 100 percent baptized or not.

My father wasn't a religious man, and I only vaguely remember him going to church once or twice with my mom and sisters as I was growing up. I'm not sure what he did on Sunday mornings when the rest of his family was at church, but his example taught me that the man of the house didn't have to go to church or assume the role of a spiritual leader.

It took me a long time to unlearn that misguided lesson. When my children were toddlers, my wife went searching for a church to attend, and I didn't always go with her. Because that's the way I was led as a child. But that soon changed as I saw my wife wanting to find more spiritual peace in her life. Having babies will do that to you. It makes you see the world in a different way. You start to realize that your role as a parent is to prepare your child for their own life.

As my children became teenagers and got more involved with the youth groups at our church, I realized that they were acting more like the religious leaders in my house than I was. They were excited about going to church. I was okay with leading the prayers at mealtime, and I was glad to go to church together, but I needed to be a stronger spiritual influence in my children's lives. I suddenly knew it was time for me to take charge as the father of the house and lead my family to Christ.

And not a moment too soon. We needed the strength of the Lord to help us through some tough times with our son.

When he became a junior high school student, my son fell in with an older group of athletes at school who led him down some wrong roads. We left the big dangerous city of Los Angeles for the safety of a small country town—only to discover that the same dangers exist everywhere. Chewing tobacco, prescription medication, alcohol—the cycle of destructive behavior was every parent's worst nightmare.

To make matters worse, one popular kid on the varsity football team soon became a negative influence on my son.

Thankfully, the Lord was with us, and even in the darkest moments of raising our son, we continued to love him and pray with him. Our son credits Christ for changing him and his destructive path. He gave up tobacco, changed his circle of friends, and continued building his faith in Christ to see him through the bad times.

Soon after, my wife and my daughter were baptized together on the same day.

A few weeks after that, my son and I were baptized together on the same day.

The proudest moment of my life as a father was watching my children being born. And then watching my whole family being born again.

I made the decision to be baptized again so that I could feel confident that I had made the choice myself. The fact that it came at the same time as my son was ready to make his decision was a tremendous blessing from the Lord.

I believe that my faith as a loving Christian father helped bring my entire family to know the Lord Jesus Christ as our personal Savior.

I made the choice to lead my children to Christ, and as a reward, I was able to lead my wife and myself there at the same time.

It's a dangerous world with many pitfalls and traps, but there's nothing like the feeling of security and safety that we have as a Christian family. The safety net that the Lord places around us can be placed around you and your family as well.

If you don't have a personal relationship with Jesus Christ and God, you will never reach your full potential in this world, and you will not have the ability to enter the kingdom of heaven. "Jesus told him 'I am the way, the truth, and the life. No one comes to the Father except through me'" (John 14:6 CSB).

There is no other way to pass from this life to heaven except through the belief in Jesus Christ, and being baptized in the name of the Father, the Son, and the Holy Spirit.

Your goal in being a loving Christian father is to lead your children to Christ through their own baptism, but how can you ever do that if you are not a believer yourself? Your faith in God will see you through all facets of your life, and your faith is your personal belief that God is real even though you can't see Him in a physical sense.

Jesus tells his disciples in John 20:29:

"Because you have seen Me, you have believed. Those who believe without seeing are blessed" (HCSB).

The facts are this. God cannot and does not lie to us. The Bible is God's Word. God tells us that the only way to achieve eternal life is through the belief in His Son Jesus Christ. You can make the decision to believe in Jesus Christ and be baptized in his blood and ascend to heaven. Or you can choose not to believe in Jesus Christ, and you will be sent to hell with the rest of the sinners of this world for all eternity.

It is your choice. You only have to ask God for forgiveness of your sins and accept Jesus Christ as your Lord and Savior, and your eternal life is guaranteed by God's promise to you and the sacrifice of His Son, Jesus Christ.

You, as a loving Christian father, must assume the role of spiritual leader for your household and family. Accept the challenge that God has in store for you and do all you can to bring your family together under His grace and guidance.

God bless you in all that you do as you go forth to make your family strong in the Lord Jesus Christ.

May you use these ten steps to be a loving Christian husband and father every day so that you and your family will earn the rewards God has placed in your life.

Amen.

www.ingramcontent.com/pod-product-compliance
Lightning Source LLC
Chambersburg PA
CBHW041627140626

46547CB00031B/1107